STAYING FOCUSED

Building Ministry Teams for Christian Formation

By M. Anne Burnette Hook and Shirley F. Clement

With contributions by Daniel T. Benedict, Jr.; Dan R. Dick; Carol F. Krau; Herb Mather; and Harmon Wray

DISCIPLESHIP RESOURCES

P.O. BOX 340003 • NASHVILLE, TN 37203-0003
www.discipleshipresources.org

Cover and book design by Joey McNair

Edited by Debra D. Smith and Cindy S. Harris

ISBN 0-88177-295-X

Library of Congress Catalog Card No. 00-108422

DR295

CONTENTS

Section One
The Purpose of Ministry Areas

When asked what the purpose of their committee or ministry team is, many leaders would respond something like, "We make sure there are ushers and greeters for worship services," or, "We recruit Sunday school teachers," or, "We monitor the heating and cooling system." While all of these tasks may be important, Section One challenges congregational leaders to look more deeply at the purpose of their ministry areas.

Chapter One

Church Committees: Task Completing or Disciple Making?

I was a newcomer to the church worship committee. The agenda was pretty typical: reports from the various area leaders, discussion about upcoming special worship days, tasks assigned to different individuals. As we were about to leave, the chairperson added, "Oh, and I would like you to pray for this family I know." It seems that a family in his daughter's school was encountering some financial and emotional difficulties. He described briefly the situation and asked us to pray for them. Then he put both hands on the table, pushed back his chair, and began to rise as if to leave. Others at the table followed his lead.

I know it sounds pious, but I spoke without thinking: "Why don't we pray right now?" The incredulous face of the chairperson indicated that I might have just sprouted another head instead of requesting that we pray. He slowly sat down and agreed. Being a good layperson, he of course asked the pastor to pray. We closed the meeting in prayer and went home.

Now, this meeting actually happened in a local United Methodist church. The members of the committee, including the chair, are active, committed laypeople. They give of their time, talents, gifts, and service to the church. The very fact that the chair asked us to pray for this family indicated his belief in prayer as an appropriate activity in the church. Why was it, then, that it was such a surprise when someone from the group suggested that we pray as a group for a particular situation right then? I suspect that while each member present would affirm a strong belief in prayer, the members had not experienced prayer as an integral part of a committee meeting before.

While I wish it were not the case, I believe that this meeting could have happened in any United Methodist church. United Methodists are known for our faith in action—the Wesleyan emphasis on "doing good of every possible sort, and, as far as possible, to all men."[1] At its best, this action is apparent in strong outreach activities, such as feeding and offering shelter for homeless people, providing food and clothes closets for families in need, building homes for the working poor, and many other acts of compassion and mercy toward those who are in need. At the conclusion of the parable of the good Samaritan, Jesus tells us to "go and do likewise" (Luke 10:37), and we very often do just that.

On the other hand, our tendency toward action has led us to be an activity-oriented church. When a new family joins your church, what is the first thing that happens to them after they've had their picture taken and have stood in a new-member line after the service? The age-old wisdom states that we get them involved, and that usually means putting them on a committee! For so many congregations, accepting new people into the life of the church means assimilation of new members. After all, resistance is futile. In other words, to get new people involved, we get them working.

Making Disciples for Christ

In 1996 the General Conference of The United Methodist Church made a historic pronouncement: that the purpose of the church is to make disciples of Jesus Christ (*The Book of Discipline—1996*; page 114). The main mission of the church is (not to make as many church members as we can but to make disciples.) In some ways this is an obvious statement; after all, Jesus' last words to his disciples were, "Go therefore and make disciples of all nations" (Matthew 28:19). Probably no one would disagree that the process of making, forming, and deploying disciples of Jesus Christ is the primary task of the church. Many churches would state most emphatically that this is exactly what they are doing.

As obvious as such a statement is, however, it is also wide open for interpretation. What exactly does it mean to make disciples? What does disciple making look like? How is it lived out in every area and activity in the local church? How does it happen in the church committee? *Does* it happen in the church committee?

The Primary Task of the Local Church

One helpful way disciple making has been expanded is through a statement of the primary task of the congregation. The 2000 *Book of Discipline of The United Methodist Church* describes disciple making as a four-part process (¶242). The four parts can be described as

- reaching out and receiving people—receiving them as they are; creating settings where people who are seeking God can be found by God, such as worship and small groups;
- relating people to God—sharing the good news of God's great love for them through Jesus Christ and God's desire to be in deeper relationship with them;
- nurturing people in discipleship—helping them understand what living as a follower of Christ involves; supporting them and encouraging them to support others through participation in small groups and outreach activities; helping them discern what their unique ministry is;
- sending people out to live as disciples in the world for the transformation of the world—helping them live out their

discipleship in their daily lives, through all of their interactions with other people, so that God uses them to touch other people's lives.

These four steps describe disciple making as a process or system in which people enter into the church seeking God, find God (or rather are found by God), grow in their understanding of what it means to be a disciple, are nurtured in and by the community, and are then sent out to be disciples in their daily lives. They are transformed by the power of the living Christ from seekers into believers and then into disciples for Christ. We in the church understand that our call is to create settings where all of this can happen. We also must work with the Spirit in the process rather than being a constraint to the process.

Jesus calls us not to assimilate members but to make disciples. This call is true for the congregation as a whole as well as for every segment of the congregation. Think about your own church and its process for making disciples. Begin with your church calendar. Look at the weekly activities listed there. What do you see that has the purpose of making disciples? Hopefully, you see corporate worship and Sunday school, Bible study classes, small groups for all ages, and various opportunities to serve others in the community.

Look once again at your weekly church calendar. What activities have a purpose other than faith formation? Finance, trustee, and other committee meetings; church athletic league practices and games; choir rehearsals; and other task-oriented or activity-oriented activities have a purpose apart from faith formation. Certainly, these activities are connected to the primary task in that they often support one of the four parts of the task. For example, without the watchful eyes of trustees maintaining the safety of the church building, creating settings where people can be welcomed and received would be more difficult. Careful preparation and presentation of worship music by the choir can help people experience God's presence in deep and profound ways. These activities can also be a faith-forming experience for those who participate, often as the byproduct of doing work for the church in the community of believers.

Look once again at the church activities that have a main purpose other than faith formation. How many are centered on Christ, and how many are centered on the institution? Or, to put it another way, how many of these activities actively and intentionally make, form, and deploy disciples, and how many focus on institutional maintenance?

Let's focus more narrowly on whatever church committee you are a part of. What is the main purpose of that committee? Is it task completion or disciple making? If the main purpose is task completion, are there opportunities for disciple making within that task completion? In short, is your committee experience a faith-forming event?

If the answer is yes, then I congratulate you and pray that as a leader of committees in the church, you will see that those on the committees you lead in the future have a similar experience. If the answer is no, I invite you to consider with me how you might make a change in your committee's life that will be transforming for the members and perhaps for the whole congregation.

Committees as Disciple-Making Experiences

I believe that people coming to our congregations are seeking experiences of the love and grace of God. The congregation as a whole, and every segment and activity in the congregation, should be about enabling people to experience God and to become disciples of Jesus Christ. If it is not, we are not being faithful to what God has called us to be. This includes the committees, who do a large part of the work of the church.

But wait, you might be thinking, if we focus on disciple making, we won't get our work done. Besides, we pray at the beginning and end of our meetings. What else do we need to do?

Disciple making in committees is much more than opening or closing with prayers or devotions. It involves an intent not just to do the work at hand but to discern what God wants that work to be. It involves shaping and forming the faith of the members on the committee in such a way that the work done together is then shaped and formed by the faith of the members. Instead of undermining or superseding the work of the committee, disciple making enhances and strengthens the work so that members feel that they are doing God's work rather than merely maintaining the institution of the church.

This kind of faith formation can happen in the committee setting. It happens when the committee chair acts as a spiritual leader for the group and intentionally uses the committee setting as a place where people can be in the presence of God. The best way to encounter God in the committee experience is through careful and intentional use of the means of grace as John Wesley has articulated them in The General Rules of The Methodist Church.

An Invitation

I invite you, as the leader of a church committee, to act as a spiritual leader of your group. This book is intended to help you explore what your committee might look like as a place where disciple making happens.

In the first part of the book, we will look at the general topic of spirituality, including current trends in spirituality and the church, how people express their individual spiritual preferences, and the means of grace as ways to both know God and experience God's presence. In the second part of the book, experts in various areas related to church committees will relate the means of grace to specific areas of church leadership: stewardship, worship, Christian education, and others. Finally, we will discuss some practical ways of incorporating these disciplines into a typical committee meeting.

You are invited to join with me in the journey. You may well be an active traveler already, or this may be a new experience for you. Perhaps you are somewhere in between the two. Wherever you are in your personal spiritual development, God is calling you to look deeper, to listen more closely, and to follow what you hear more faithfully. God is also calling you, as a leader of others, to entice others into the journey by both the example of your own walk and your intentional leadership of a church committee.

If you desire to be more than just a committee chair that gets the job done and to also be a spiritual leader for the committee, I encourage you to pray as you read this book. Trust that God will work through the Holy Spirit and show you how your committee's life and work together might become a disciple-making, faith-forming experience.

Endnote

1 From "The General Rules of The Methodist Church," in *The Book of Discipline of The United Methodist Church—2000*. Copyright © 2000 by The United Methodist Publishing House. Used by permission; page 73.

Chapter Two

Spirituality Is IN!

Some polls by Gallup and others seem to indicate that people in the United States are starting to look beyond the material to the spiritual. They are realizing that the capitalistic, search-for-the-American-dream existence may be closer to a nightmare than to a dream, or at least has not lived up to its hype. This renewed interest in spiritual things is a tremendous opportunity for the church to reach out to those seeking a fuller, more meaningful life. "The fields are ripe for harvesting" (John 4:35) in ways they haven't been before.

The down side to this situation is that the church has already lost many of these people who are seeking a meaningful experience of God. Some have turned (or returned) to mainline Protestant denominations in the last decade for answers to their meaning-of-life questions. But many have also left the church again after not finding what they were looking for. Although the church seems the logical place to search for such answers, the church has unfortunately not always known what to do with seekers other than get them involved in the institution. You're looking for God? We put you on a committee. In worship, the practices of traditional church worship do not always allow for experiences of God outside the narrow order of the worship bulletin. In addition, people who do experience God in vital ways often do not find places to share their experiences within traditional church settings. Indeed the goal of institutional Christianity for the last several decades seems to have focused more on church membership and church growth than on discipleship and spirituality. As a result, seekers have turned away from the church for guidance and to a variety of spiritualities ranging from cultural sects to New Age groups.

Fortunately, there is more good news for the church. The message of the church, the good news of Jesus Christ, is still relevant and exciting to those who are seeking God. It is up to the church to refocus its attention on making disciples instead of on making members. If we are to help people go deeper than whatever self-help program The Church of What's Happening Now is offering, we must help them understand that they can find what they are seeking in a deep and meaningful relationship with the living God. And we must see that our churches offer ways of developing and nurturing such a relationship in all of its activities and programs, including its ministry area work. What is ironic is that the most effective way to help contemporary people come to this relationship in this day and age is a return to our roots: practicing the traditional spiritual disciplines, also known as the means of grace.

What Are the Means of Grace?

The means of grace may seem too theological for many to understand. The words *means of grace* seem easy enough. A means is a way to get something or to get someplace, an approach or a method. Sometimes the word refers to money or the lack thereof, as when someone lacks the means to purchase something. Sometimes it refers to a method, often undesirable or at least questionable, used to achieve a desirable result, as in *the end justifies the means.* Grace is that which we have received from God, the unconditional love God offers us in spite of our many failings. Grace comes to us as we receive the love God offers and gratefully respond to that love with lives of service to God. So the means of grace are those methods that enable us to both receive and respond to the love offered to us from God.

Another name for the means of grace is *the traditional spiritual disciplines*. That name sounds more like a punishment than a way of being in a closer relationship with God. At its worst, the name calls forth images of isolated monks torturing themselves in order to make themselves more pure, holy, and acceptable before God. At the least, it sounds like one more "ought" in a long list of self-help tasks that we need to add to our "to do" list, somewhere between working out at the gym for an hour and serving dinner at a homeless shelter. It hardly sounds like a way for Christians to be in a more meaningful relationship with God.

However confusing or off-putting the name *means of grace* may sound to modern ears, the means of grace are ways that people have been in closer relationship with God throughout the centuries. These practices offer Christians specific methods to "know [God] more clearly, love [God] more dearly, and follow [God] more nearly," as an ancient prayer goes (Richard of Chichester, England, thirteenth century). And, as overwhelming as taking on a new set of spiritual disciplines may seem, it helps to remember that the goal is both knowing more about who God is and being in a closer relationship with God, not mastering new skills and disciplines.

What are these means to a deeper knowledge of and relationship with God? There are many different ways that we can experience God's grace. Some means of grace are appropriate as general rules of life for all Christians. Some have been ordained by God through the Scriptures as means to encounter and participate in the presence of God in all ages and for all Christians. Other means vary according to each person in each generation. Although means of grace have been practiced by Christians from the beginning of Christianity, they are closely associated with John Wesley, founder of the Methodist movement.

Wesley, an ordained Anglican priest, was dismayed at what he observed as a lackluster commitment to God and little practice of what God ordained among the members of his church. His answer for his own life was to form small groups of individuals who were convinced of their own sinfulness and desired to lead a more holy life. They made a covenant with one another and God to practice the means of grace in their daily lives. They met regularly to hold one another accountable for their journey. Their discipline was so methodical that they were nicknamed Methodists. Wesley wrote a famous sermon on the means of grace that is now required reading for most United Methodist seminary students. He also clearly spelled out the means of grace in The General Rules of The Methodist Church (*The Book of Discipline—2000*; pages 71–74.)

Do No Harm and Avoid Evil

The first means of grace that Wesley described in the General Rules is to do no harm and to avoid evil of all kinds. Wesley included several things to avoid that were applicable to Wesley's day and age, when the rules were first written. These included drunkenness, taking the Lord's name in vain, slaveholding, not observing the sabbath, fighting with others, being deceitful in business dealings, borrowing that which you do not intend to return, wearing lots of costly garments, and hoarding earthly treasures. Today we can easily apply the rule to most of these same evils, for they still exist even in our so-called enlightened society. Some of these evils are individual sins, things that individuals do to harm one another. Others are institutional evils, systems and practices in institutions (including the church) that oppress people and treat them as less than created and loved children of God. Part of our discipline as faithful Christians is to clearly name those acts and attitudes that are incompatible with Christian teachings and to discipline ourselves and caution others to avoid doing those things.

Naming the harmful, evil acts and attitudes present in our world is a difficult and tricky task. Our pluralistic society is careful not to judge questionable behavior as anything other than different.

Sin is out; individual freedom is in. This freedom is held as the highest standard, sometimes over the needs of the whole society. Naming behavior that is evil is indeed a bold and risky thing to do. It is bold because doing so is unpopular. It is risky because it is all too easy to see the speck in someone else's eye, all the time avoiding the log in our own eye, as Jesus pointed out (Luke 6:41).

If this first general rule is so difficult to accomplish, then how can Christians, who are also fallible humans, hope to do this? The only real way to avoid being hypocritical and judgmental is to faithfully practice other spiritual disciplines so that we are in tune with the God who helps us see and do what is good and right, and name and avoid what is evil.

Do Good of Every Kind

The second means of grace that Wesley described is to do good of every kind. Here Wesley referred first to tending to the needs of others, both physical and spiritual. Then he called all Christians to obedience, denying themselves, and taking up their crosses daily.

Fortunately, doing good for others is a common practice in our society. Participation in civic organizations may be less common than it used to be, but doing good is still considered a worthy occupation of time. Certainly churches continue answering the call of Christ to be in ministry with and for those on the margins of our society. They offer everything from meals, shelter, and clothing to financial counseling and job search aid for homeless people, as well as welcoming these people into their church homes as guests and members. Doing good is not a hard concept to sell.

Self-denial, on the other hand, is not a popular undertaking. Instant gratification seems to be the favorite hobby of our society. Consumer debt is way up; individual savings are way down. We commonly see instant coffee, instant oatmeal, and instant credit; meals you can heat and eat in your car; ads for taking off thirty pounds in thirty days. You name it, we want it—and we want it now.

Compare that with Jesus' repeated teaching: "If any want to become my followers, let them deny themselves and take up their cross and follow me" (Matthew 16:24, Mark 8:34, Luke 9:23). The concept of taking up a cross has been twisted and misunderstood over the years. Some say they have a "cross to bear," meaning an unwanted burden placed on them by someone else. Others, in an attempt to comfort someone with a significant burden, have contributed to the confusion by not only agreeing with the assessment but adding the out-of-context quotation that God doesn't give us anything we can't handle.

In the Bible passage quoted above, Jesus did not mean by "take up their cross" having to bear burdens placed upon us by God or by others in the name of faithfulness. Rather, taking up our cross is an intentional choice to pick up and carry a specific load so as to participate in the suffering of Christ. An extreme example of this concept is the life and ministry of Mother Teresa, who lived her life in ministry with the poor and sick of Calcutta because she saw in each of these people's eyes the face of Christ. No one forced her to live in this manner; she willingly chose to as a response to God's love for her and call to act. Other more common examples are people who choose to live a simple lifestyle so that they can give more to those in need, teachers who remain in low-paying positions because of their commitment to the education of others, and many others who make daily choices of self-denial. They do these things, not because someone else forces them to or to score points with God, but because they feel called by God to do these things; and in being obedient, they enhance their relationship with God.

Attend to the Ordinances of God

The third means of grace outlined in the General Rules is to attend to the ordinances of God, participating in those things that God has asked all faithful Christians to do. These ordinances are described in the following sections.

Public Worship of God

Attending worship in our day is often seen as something nice to do rather than as a sign of obedient living for God. Gallup polls

20

indicate that around ninety-five percent of Americans believe in God, and that about eighty percent call themselves Christians. Yet only about forty percent of American people are in worship on any given week, and only about thirty percent regularly attend every week. These statistics indicate that worship attendance is considered by many a non-essential part of being a Christian.

In spite of current trends and opinions, public worship is still the main event in the life of the church. It is the one time when all of the community gathers together in praise of the One who gave us life and gives us new life. Worship is when we remember what God has done, both for us and in all of human history. We retell the stories of faith from the Bible, and we rehearse our relationship with God as individuals and as a community. We praise God for all God has done and all God will do and, to echo the psalmist, because God "is worthy to be praised" (Psalm 18:3a). Public worship allows us to step outside our own self-absorbed existence to see the bigger picture: that God, who loves and cares about me, is the God of all the universe and all of history. Even if we gather in different congregations at different times of the week with different music, rituals, styles of preaching, and dress codes, we are truly one body as we worship the living God together.

John Wesley understood the power of public worship. He preached salvation from tree stumps in the middle of the week to bring the good news to those who did not attend church, but every week he attended worship in the Anglican Church. Even Jesus, who personified relationship with God, understood the importance of regular public worship in our relationship with God: "When he came to Nazareth, where he had been brought up, he went to the synagogue on the sabbath day, as was his custom" (Luke 4:16). Worship of God is essential to a deep and abiding relationship with God, for it allows us to both hear about and acknowledge with praise who God truly is.

Observance of Holy Communion

This practice goes hand-in-hand with worship because it happens in the context of worship. For John Wesley, an Anglican who would have celebrated Holy Communion each sabbath day as part of the service, the two may have been inseparable. However, when the Methodist faith headed across the Atlantic and on to the shores of the New World and the new United States, the absence of ordained clergy necessitated the separation of Holy Communion from weekly public worship. In addition, the camp meeting of the Methodist movement focused on salvation and personal commitment to Jesus. In such meetings, the sermon was central. After the Methodists moved from the campgrounds into the sanctuaries, the worship order remained more heavily influenced by our frontier upbringing than by our Anglican roots. Today, many United Methodist congregations celebrate Holy Communion once a month.

There is anecdotal evidence (meaning a lot of people talk about it but there is little hard research to support it) that worship attendance drops on Communion Sundays. If this is true, it may be due to a longer-than-usual service on Communion Sundays. Other reasons may be that the Communion liturgy in the recent past focused on the sacrificial nature of Table rather than the celebration of God's action in our lives. Some people have grown up believing that they must be "worthy" and without sin in order to receive the Lord's Supper. Certainly, God wants us to acknowledge and confess our sin; however, if we were to wait to come to the Lord's Table until we actually deserved it, we would never receive the graceful meal intended as a gift from God.

The language in the ritual in *The United Methodist Hymnal* better reflects the thanksgiving we may feel when we receive this gift. This is why many people call this celebration the Eucharist, which literally means thanksgiving. The Prayer of Great Thanksgiving itself recalls God's mighty acts throughout all of history, culminating in God's gift of Jesus (*Hymnal*; pages 9 and 10). It helps us remember once again how God saved us and continues to save us. It reminds us that we are to be the body of Christ for the world, in grateful response to all God has done for us. When celebrated, and not merely endured, receiving the Holy Meal on a regular basis is indeed a powerful way to strengthen our relationship with God by reminding us of all God is and has done.

Prayer

Prayer can be private, family, or public. It can be written or spoken. Of the ordinances listed by John Wesley as means of grace, prayer is probably the one practice most Christians are comfortable with. We pray to thank God for specific blessings, to acknowledge the power of God, to ask for forgiveness, and to request help for specific needs.

Prayer is what enables us to keep in regular contact with God. As with human relationships, a deep and meaningful relationship with God requires time spent in the presence of God and conversation with God. It cannot thrive and grow on a mumbled word here or there in times of trouble. Unlike the man who, upon hearing his wife's complaint that he never told her he loved her, replied, "I told you once; when I change my mind I'll let you know," a full relationship with God requires more intentional contact than that. Prayer is a way to be in relationship with God.

There are many different types of prayer. John Wesley names several in the General Rules: private, public, family; written and spoken. Most Christians today would probably not categorize prayers in this manner. However, doing so and looking at different ways of praying may help us discover whole new ways of knowing and being in relationship with God.

There are volumes of worthy reading on the subject of prayer. In this space, I mention only some of the ways of praying that are common and easily practiced. Prayer as conversation, in which we offer to God our thanks as well as our concerns, is the most familiar form of praying. But there are others that also help us draw closer to God and hear God's word for us and our ministry.

Meditative prayer is another, more focused form of praying. This form, where the person focuses on a word or thought rather than forming words and sentences to God, is especially appropriate when words are hard to come by or unnecessary. When practiced individually, meditation helps people focus, relax, and rest comfortably in the presence of God. In groups, meditation prayer may be appropriate when there is a decision to be made and discernment from the Spirit is needed.

Praying a Scripture passage is another form of prayer. Different from studying the Scriptures, it allows us to place ourselves in the Bible narrative, perhaps giving us a new perspective.

Journaling is a form of written prayer that helps us focus our thoughts and concerns. Even though these written thoughts may not be shared with others, for many this writing of spiritual things helps clarify and focus our thinking on God things rather than our own thing.

It is tempting, particularly in a ministry area or committee meeting, to use "bookend praying," that is, a prayer at the beginning, a prayer at the end, and business as usual in the middle. Part of the challenge in practicing the means of grace as a methodical, spiritual lifestyle is to break away from the business as usual and invite God to speak to us in between the bookends.

Just as individual prayer can and does influence our daily lives as Christians as well as enhance our relationship with God, so prayer in and around ministry area meetings and work can and does influence our decisions and enhance our lives together as servants in ministry.

Scripture Study

Scripture study includes reading Scripture, meditating upon Scripture, or hearing the Scripture proclaimed. Studying the Word of God contained in the Bible is perhaps the most central way to learn more about the God we worship. Through the pages of the Bible we come to know the mighty acts of God throughout history. Recorded in the pages of this book are accounts of creation; God's covenants with God's people; the life, death, and resurrection of Jesus Christ; the birth and spread of the early church; and the promise of God's eternal reign in the fullness of time. However, it is much more than a history book. Not only does it tell of God's mighty acts of salvation throughout history, but it also provides us with a blueprint for how we can participate in that reign and help bring about God's kingdom here on earth now. It not only offers us a guide to who God is but also helps us experience God in our lives.

The experiences of the people in the Bible mirror our own experiences in many ways. The Bible is a record of humanity's growing awareness and understanding of, and finally belief in, the God of all creation. The people in the Bible had many of the same problems we have. They coped with issues of life and death, with anger and joy, with famine and plenty. They were sometimes supremely faithful to God's requirements of them; often they failed miserably. Yet through it all God remained faithful. If God can choose a man like Samson, or a young teenage girl like Mary, or an extremist like Saul to be God's agents on earth, can God not also call all of us to live as agents of grace and justice in our own families and communities?

John Wesley understood the Bible to be the primary source for those wishing to live a life of grace. Wesley believed that careful Scripture study helps avoid the extremes of exclusively intellectual or personal religious experiences. The Bible challenges those who are tempted to understand God only through their own personal experience ("just me and Jesus") to see God's acts in broader terms. The Bible's call to take up your cross and follow Jesus challenges the complacent "head" religion of those who are tempted to know all about God but not live a life according to Jesus' teachings. True discipleship involves both knowing God's identity and personally experiencing God's presence on a daily basis. Scripture study helps us do both.

Christian Conferencing

Also referred to as Christian conversation, Christian conferencing is fellowship with other believers in order to attend to spiritual growth, or conversations that introduce unbelievers to God and what God has done. Although Christian conferencing was not included in the General Rules, Wesley named it as a means of grace in other writings.

Christian conversation happens when we talk with one another about our experiences with the means of grace, such as gleaning an insight from Scripture study, asking for prayer support for a particular problem, or offering a praise to God in worship. It also happens when we ask the important question, What do we feel called by God to do in this situation?

Christian conferencing can help clarify our mission and goals as the church of the living Christ. Instead of focusing on the needs of the institutional church, such conversations help us see beyond our own limited view of the community around us to the community as God sees it. It enables us to hear more clearly what God is calling us to do, and to act in ways more in keeping with that call.

Fasting or Abstinence

Fasting is temporarily giving up physical sustenance in order to make us aware of our dependence upon God alone and to remove barriers that may keep us from experiencing God's presence. John Wesley thought this was such an important means of grace that he called on all Methodists to fast on Wednesdays and Fridays.

In our day, fasting is not exactly a common activity, at least not for religious reasons. We are more familiar with people who fast as a type of fad diet or as a political statement of protest. We may associate fasting with excessive religious practices of years gone by, and we try to avoid anything that will make us uncomfortable. In a society when we are encouraged to get what we want when we want it, fasting is not a desirable activity.

Many who are quick to dismiss this practice as irrelevant in our day do not realize that fasting has been a commonly practiced spiritual discipline in every century but our own. Biblical characters such as Moses, David, Esther, Zechariah, and even Jesus himself observed days of fasting. The disciples fasted after Jesus had ascended into heaven. Other church leaders throughout the ages have practiced regular fast days.

Fasting in its most literal meaning is abstaining from eating food in solid or liquid forms for a period of time. The focus of fasting is spiritual. Although some may fast for political gain (as in a hunger strike to influence a government's public policy) or to get rid of those pesky unwanted holiday pounds, true fasting is a spiritual discipline. The end in fasting is a deeper relationship with and understanding of God, not some otherworldly end such as political power or physical leanness.

The purpose of fasting, then, is to deny ourselves something that we often take for granted so that we may focus on God as the source of all good gifts in our lives, even the very food that we eat. The hunger pangs we experience are reminders of God's gracious gifts in our lives. Hunger becomes a prayer of thanks to God and an acute reminder that there are many in our world who feel these pangs daily. Denying ourselves something so basic as food helps us to take the focus away from fulfilling our every want and need and to focus on those things that God is calling us to consider and tend to.

Many of us are afraid of fasting. We fear how we will feel physically; we fear how others will perceive us. We may secretly fear that we could easily do without that which seems so important today. We are so obsessed with taking care of number one that we forget to rely on the One who knows and provides for our every need even before we can name it. In our frantic pursuit of all we want and think we need, we cannot hear the call of God to care for those for whom God has a special love, those who do not have the very basic provisions of life and are on the margins of society.

Fasting can take us out of our own self-absorbed lives into a deeper relationship with God and love for God's people. It can cleanse our insides and sharpen our focus on God's desires for us rather than our own desires for ourselves. It reminds us to spend more time providing for those who cannot provide for themselves.

Fasting is not restricted to abstaining from food. We can fast from many activities that keep us from being the people God has called us to be, including behaviors that diminish our relationship with God and others.

Because fasting is an individual discipline, it is probably not an activity that many ministry groups or committees will observe often. (Also, fasting may not be recommended for people with some physical conditions, such as diabetes.) However, historically in times of great crisis, groups have participated in a time of fasting and prayer to call upon God for help and strength. As group members feel led to practice this discipline individually, they may tell the group of their experiences as a witness. Listen to God's word on this practice as a way of being in deeper and fuller relationship with God, and allow the Holy Spirit to guide your group's decisions regarding fasting.

The Means of Grace Today

These means of grace have enabled Christians throughout history to both know about and understand more fully the God we worship, as well as to experience the presence of God in our daily lives. A current model for group life practicing the means of grace is evident in Covenant Discipleship Groups. These small groups, modeled after the early Methodist class meeting, challenge members to return to Wesley's methodical practice of the means of grace as a way of living more faithful, holy lives.

The Christian is called to works of mercy, which include acts of compassion (helping those on the margins of society have their most basic needs met) and acts of justice (addressing the injustices of the system that allows people to be on the margins, Christian conversation). In addition, the Christian is also called to works of piety, which include acts of devotion (prayer, searching the Scripture, fasting) and acts of worship (worship, the Lord's supper). These four areas of ministry and piety are held in tension with one another. Members of Covenant Discipleship Groups write a group covenant that all members agree to uphold. The covenant clearly spells out what the expectations of each member are. The covenant is used as a way for members to hold themselves and one another accountable for their spiritual growth.

Apart from those people who participate in Covenant Discipleship Groups, are the traditional means of grace really relevant in our church today? Aren't there other ways (means) through which we experience God's love and grace? Of course; yet God has chosen throughout history to relate to us primarily through the means of grace outlined in the General Rules. They inform us about who God is by retelling the mighty acts of God in history. They enable us to experience God personally through acts of prayer, worship, and service to others. Without experience of and understanding of God at work in our world and our lives, how could we differentiate between an encounter with the God of all creation and an encounter with the god of our own creation?

However important and vital the means are to a deeper relationship with God, the means are not the end. It would be easy to think of these means as a measuring stick of our faithfulness as Christians: If we attend worship regularly, pray daily alone and with our families, do all the good we can, and avoid evil at every turn, we somehow have made it as Christians. That attitude misses the point entirely. We cannot pray enough, worship enough, do enough good, or avoid enough evil to earn God's love. The grace offered to us has already been given, before or even whether we respond. The means of grace are ways that we are in relationship with the One who created us and loves us. They help us know who the God is whom we worship, what God has done and will do, and how we can participate in God by living as faithful disciples. The means are not the ends; the end is relationship with Love itself, the living God.

Means of Grace and Different Spiritual Types

As you think about the various members of your congregation, you may think about them according to their individual ministry preferences. John is head of the outreach committee because of his strong call to social action. He is often not in worship because he is serving meals at a local soup kitchen. Susan is on the education committee because she is committed to Christian education for all ages. Jan's contemplative nature and active prayer life led her to organize a churchwide prayer chain. Mark's experience with a weekend spiritual renewal retreat prompted him to organize and lead an alternative praise and worship service as part of the church's spiritual formation offerings.

Each of these people has a deep relationship with God; each simply shapes his or her response to that relationship in a different way. These people have different spiritual preferences, and you and the people in your congregation do as well. Many people will self-select particular areas of ministry by their agreeing to work on various work areas and committees.

What are the different spiritual preferences, and how do they manifest themselves in the life of the church? In her book *Discover Your Spiritual Type* (see page 94), Dr. Corinne Ware explores four spiritual types: head spirituality, heart spirituality, mystic spirituality, and kingdom spirituality. These are not stereotypes with which to label people; they are preferences that help us understand how people relate to God more easily.

The head spirituality is an intellectual faith. People with this spiritual preference favor thoughtful, reasonable sermons; well-crafted hymn texts; and theologically sound prayers. Pastors with this spiritual preference will choose a hymn that the congregation does not know because it expresses a specific idea addressed in the sermon. Congregation members with this spiritual preference would probably choose to participate in Bible studies that emphasize a scholarly approach, church committees such as education, and other church activities that engage their brains.

The heart spirituality is more concerned with emotions than intellect. The primary religious interests of people with this spiritual preference are evangelism, witnessing, and testimonies. The focus tends to be more on the personal experience of God rather than on the corporate expression of praise to God. People with this type of spirituality value emotional experience over doctrinal purity, and they don't feel that they have worshiped unless they experience an emotional response.

The head spirituality and heart spirituality are two different ways of being in relationship with God. Sometimes the differences between the two create conflicts within a committed and thoughtful Christian. I once had a conversation with a colleague about her church's worship. She is a member of a large United Methodist congregation with a traditional, formal worship service. She said, "I love my church. The choir is magnificent. The preaching is very good. The worship service is well crafted, and the ministers are effective leaders. It absolutely leaves me cold." She was describing the tension between the church's head spirituality worship experience and her own heart spirituality preference. Neither is right or wrong; they are merely preferences.

Conflicts among different spiritual types can emerge within congregations as well. Each spiritual type tends to believe that theirs is the best way to reach God. For example, head and heart spiritualities believe that God is knowable; they just know God through different means. This can cause mild conflicts at the least and church schisms at the most! The head spirituality is tempted to say to the heart spirituality, "My theology is purer that yours," and the heart spirituality retorts, "Oh, yeah? Well, my walk with the Lord is closer than yours!" Again, it helps to remember that one does not bring people closer to God. They are individual preferences based on how we experience and relate to God.

Two other spiritual types are also apparent but in fewer numbers in local churches than the first two described. One is mystic spirituality. The mystic prefers to experience God, as does the heart spirituality; but this experience is of the mystery of God rather than what we can know about God through our experience. Those who prefer mystic spirituality focus on hearing from God rather than talking to God. Silence is often the music of the mystics. Because this type of spirituality attracts those for whom solitude is a better means of experiencing God, there are fewer mystics in the organized church, particularly in mainline Protestant congregations. However, their presence is invaluable to those of us who are into a head spirituality, because they help us stretch beyond what we can know about God and into the mysteries of what we cannot know.

A fourth spiritual type is the kingdom spirituality. People with this type of spirituality see their whole lives as their prayer. Social concerns and justice issues top the list for them. This group is the least likely to participate in organized institutional religious activities, because they perceive in these congregations a lack of concern about the things they hold most sacred. When they are present, they are often the leaders of the church's outreach program, and they are among the first to urge members to political and social action.

Why is noting different spiritual types important? First, it helps us better understand how we relate to God and which activities and disciplines will bring us closer to God. As we contemplate increasing our contact with God, we are more likely to be consistent in our journey if we use means that are more comfortable to us, especially if we are new to the journey. Knowing our spiritual preferences enables us to accept ourselves as spiritual beings who relate best to God in a particular way.

Second, knowing about different spiritual types allows us to see the areas in which we might stretch in order to experience a fuller, more integrated picture of God. God is so much broader than any one person's experience, or God wouldn't be God. Testing new ways of encountering our Creator broadens our own experience and helps us appreciate other people's experiences of God. If you tend to experience God with a head spirituality, a quiet retreat for contemplation will increase your ability to listen to God in the midst of your busy life. If heart spirituality is more comfortable for you, some experience helping the poor, such as a week-long mission trip into the poor counties of Appalachia or tutoring a child from a low-income family in math every week, would expand your appreciation for those whom God has special affection, those on the margins of our society.

Finally, knowing about different spiritual types enables us to be more understanding and tolerant of other people's spiritualities, especially people with whom we provide some spiritual leadership, for example the ministry areas we lead. Because of our spiritual preferences, each of us tends to focus more on specific means of grace rather than to practice all the means in a disciplined way. Some of us may even believe, just a little, that our way of being in relationship with God is really the best way. Appreciating that people experience God in different ways will help you be a more balanced spiritual leader to those you lead.

Implications for Ministry Areas

I can hear the resistance now: "But, I'm new to the faith." "I'm just a layperson. I'm not a pastor." Or even, "Hey, I just signed up to chair this committee! How can I be a spiritual leader?" These are certainly honest and appropriate reactions.

Let's start with where you are now. If you are the leader of a ministry area, you are a leader—the leader of that group. You may have little or lots of leadership training. You may be an expert or novice at moving a group toward a common goal. Regardless of your training and skills, you are already a leader in the eyes of those who work under your direction. The question now is whether you will choose to be a spiritual leader.

God wants to be in closer relationship with you. When you intentionally choose to respond to that invitation, you open yourself to the spiritual life. As you grow and learn in that relationship, as you practice the means of grace in your daily life, you grow in faith. As you use what you have experienced and learned in your work with a ministry area, you exercise your spiritual leadership of the group.

For example, people who have experienced the power of intercessory prayers will build into the group meetings an opportunity for the members to pray for others. People who have wrestled with Scripture in the midst of daily devotions will share their learnings as a way of preparing the group for tasks they face. They will also invite further reflection from the other members, since spiritual leaders know that they do not have all the answers. Ministry area leaders who are also spiritual leaders will create a setting in the committee meetings where disciples can be made and formed in the midst of the work of the church.

Does it take a seminary degree to be a spiritual leader? No, just the willingness to be on the journey and invite others onto the journey with you. Your personal journey will involve the regular practice of the means of grace. Your role as spiritual leader will include the incorporation of the means of grace in the ministry area meetings as a way of introducing and encouraging the spiritual growth of those you lead. The invitation that is open to you is open to all: to be in closer and deeper relationship with God. The means of grace offer us the best way to respond to that invitation, both personally and corporately.

You may still have questions, such as, I'm chair of the finance (worship, education, outreach, fill-in-the-blank) committee. I thought all that spiritual stuff was for the spiritual formation groups. Why am I supposed to do that as well? This too is an appropriate question to ask. We as a church have functioned pretty well, or so we like to think, with the mentality that if all the separate parts work, then we are fulfilling the task of the church, making disciples of Jesus Christ. So we have divided up all the various tasks—evangelism, worship, stewardship, outreach, education, spiritual formation, and the rest—with the idea that if each part does its own job well, then the task is done, the kingdom comes, and we can all go home.

Time has shown us that churches don't really accomplish the mission of the church by dividing up the various parts of that mission among groups. If the mission of the church is making disciples for Jesus Christ, every part of the church needs to be about this task. All of the activities the church is engaged in are secondary to this one mission. The church is a system for disciple making.

What does it mean to refer to the church as a disciple-making system? Systems theory is prominent in business and other arenas in today's world and is too complex to flesh out completely. However, the following example may make the basics clear.

A dishwasher is a system for cleaning dishes. Dirty dishes are put into the washer. Detergent, water, and electricity are added. A certain action of the water and detergent causes the dirt to be removed from the dishes. If the dishes are really dirty, the power wash button can be pushed and another action works on that tough, dried-on food. Another action, the drying cycle, uses heat to dry the dishes. If everything works correctly, clean dishes are left.

What if you had a dishwasher that was great at drying the dishes but added no water? You would get dirty dishes with dried-on food that only the most powerful dishwasher could then remove. What if you had no electricity? You would have dirty dishes in a useless dishwasher. Only when each part of the system works is the mission of the system achieved.

Another example may be even more appropriate for churches. Many church choirs sing four-part choral harmonies. Few choirs achieve total balance among these four parts. Most choirs have more sopranos and few tenors, or lots of basses and not enough strong altos. It would be ridiculous to suggest that if the director can get the sopranos to sing their part perfectly, at the same time ignoring the other three parts, the anthem will be all that the director hopes it will be. In order to achieve the mission of presenting a beautiful, four-part anthem for worship, each part must be engaged and working together.

In the same way, it is not enough to divide the tasks of disciple making into functional committees responsible for each smaller part. When that happens some parts may function well, but the mission of the church will likely not be achieved. You may have a tremendous outreach program; but if it does not fully participate in the church's mission, it is not doing the true mission of the church, which is to make, nurture, and send out disciples for Jesus Christ. Your finances may be in such good order that an auditor would pay you for the privilege of looking at your records; but if the finance and stewardship ministries of the church do not help make disciples, they are not living up to the task. Only when the whole church is about making disciples can we hope to fulfill that awesome task.

Your mission, then, is to lead your ministry area so that it participates in the making, nurturing, and sending forth of disciples. It is a tough job, probably different from what you signed on to do. It may mean doing business in a new way, leaving time at meetings for study of relevant Scriptures, prayer, and Christian conversation. It will definitely require some careful and prayerful thought about what it means to be a disciple and where you are in your personal relationship with God. It may require you to talk about that relationship with others as well as to encourage them to join you on this journey. You will also need to carefully balance doing and being—getting the work of the team done as well as nurturing each other in the faith. That's an awful lot of work for a volunteer position in the church.

However daunting this task may seem, you have resources available to help you with it. In the following sections, experts in various areas of ministry give ideas for incorporating the means of grace into your particular ministry area. Read your particular area first, then consider your own response to their suggestions. Share those ideas with members of your ministry team, and ask for their feedback. Read the other sections as well for insight they may offer to your own area.

Remember too that you do not go on this journey alone. You walk with the other members of your ministry team as well as the other spiritual leaders in your congregation who lead groups. And you walk with God, who calls us into ministry and gives us exactly what we need to fulfill that call.

Section Two
Getting Specific

A new, more flexible organization for the local church was written into the 1996 *Book of Discipline of The United Methodist Church*. Fewer offices were mandated. The broad ministry areas became nurture (education, stewardship, worship); outreach (advocacy concerns, justice ministries, community and global mission); and witness (evangelism, spiritual formation, communications, membership care, Lay Speaking Ministries). Finance responsibilities, care of facilities, and a committee on lay leadership are also part of the basic organization. Other teams may be formed as the congregation sees necessary for carrying out the mission of making disciples of Jesus Christ.

Section Two contains suggestions for those who lead these lay ministry teams. You may want to read sections other than the one that relates to your specific area of spiritual leadership. The information will help you and your ministry team design your time together as a time of disciple making and faith formation as well as a time of doing your task for ministry out of a biblical and theological foundation.

Chapter Three

Administrative Ministry Areas: Committee on Lay Leadership

"Like good stewards of the manifold grace of God, serve one another with whatever gift each of you has received" (1 Peter 4:10). How do these words define the work and intention of a committee on lay leadership (formerly the committee on nominations and personnel)?

The Book of Discipline of The United Methodist Church defines the work of a committee on lay leadership to be "to identify, develop, deploy, evaluate, and monitor Christian spiritual leadership for the local congregation."[1]

As your team begins its work together, discuss the following questions:

1. How can we help people discover their spiritual gifts?
2. How can we help people better understand their spiritual gifts and develop their skills for ministry and service?
3. What kind of training will we need to improve our ministries in support of our mission?
4. What resources will be most helpful for training and evaluation?

5. How does the discovery, development, and deployment of gifted spiritual leaders help us fulfill the mission of our church?
6. How can we model gifted leadership grounded firmly in spiritual discipline and practice?

The work of a committee on lay leadership is, first and foremost, spiritual work. It is imperative that "members of the committee shall engage in and be attentive to developing and enhancing their own Christian spiritual life in light of the mission of the Church."[2] Practice of the Wesleyan means of grace is an excellent way for this committee to prepare for its vital work.

Prayer

It was Wesley's expectation that Christian people—especially those entrusted with the leadership of the congregation—would regularly and intentionally pray together. Jesus' injunction that "whatever you ask for in prayer with faith, you will receive" (Matthew 21:22) and Paul's admonition to "pray without ceasing" (1 Thessalonians 5:17) are of critical importance to the life and work of the church.

These questions can help guide the committee as it develops its prayer life:
1. As members of the committee on lay leadership, what kind of guidance and insight should we be praying for?
2. In order to be effective in ministry, we need people. How often should we pray about and for the people we need?
3. What is our commitment to pray for one another as we work together to provide solid spiritual leadership for our congregation?

Scripture Study

A second means of grace beneficial to a committee on lay leadership is the study of Scripture. Studying God's Word together opens new dimensions of understanding. Three passages of Scripture are especially valuable for study by the committee on lay leadership. They are Romans 12, 1 Corinthians 12, and Ephesians

4:1-16. You may want to devote three meetings to the study of these passages. Each focuses on the nature of our life together as the church, centered in the gifts of the Spirit.

Use the questions in the chart below and on page 42 to guide personal reflection and group discussion for each passage.

Scripture	Questions for Reflection
Romans 12	1. What does it mean to present our bodies to God as a living sacrifice? 2. How do we discern the will of God? 3. How does the metaphor of the church as a body apply to our congregation? How well do we know and understand one another's gifts? 4. What would need to change or happen in our church to enable us to live by Paul's instructions in Romans 12:9-21? How can we make this kind of Christian living easier for one another? 5. How does our learning from Romans 12 inform this committee's work?
1 Corinthians 12	1. How are spiritual gifts different from interests, talents, or abilities? 2. How does 1 Corinthians 12 build on the metaphor of the body? How healthy is our congregational body at the moment? Where are the areas of greatest health and vitality? Where is there illness or weakness? 3. Compare the list of gifts in 1 Corinthians 12:27-31 with the list in Romans 12:6-8. What are the similarities? What are the differences? Why might the lists differ? 4. How does our learning from 1 Corinthians 12 inform this committee's work?

Scripture	Questions for Reflection
Ephesians 4:1-16	1. Why are spiritual gifts important? What are they given for?
	2. How does our congregation help people live out of their spiritual gifts? Where do we see people using their gifts in and beyond our congregation? What can we do to help people develop their gifts?
	3. Compare the list of gifts in Ephesians 4 with the lists from the Corinthians and Romans passages. What do you notice about these lists?
	4. How does our learning from Ephesians 4 inform this committee's work?

Having explored the Scriptures together, prayerfully reflect on and discuss the following questions in light of your learning about spiritual gifts:

1. Who are the people who possess the appropriate gifts to carry out specific ministries? (worship, stewardship, education, outreach, healing, evangelism, missions, and so forth)
2. What gifts do people possess that could enable us to develop new ministries? What gifts do people possess that might be used to extend our ministry beyond our current program?
3. What gifts do we possess that we can use to serve our community?
4. How can we better assist people in using their spiritual gifts beyond the church?

Fasting

An overlooked and misunderstood spiritual practice is that of fasting. Throughout history, fasting has been a means of focusing on the will of God and sacrificing self-sufficiency. Many people report that they think more clearly, feel more deeply, and gain clear intuition when they fast. The committee on lay leadership may want to fast quarterly or monthly as they gather together to select leaders for the work of the church. Reflect on these questions as a committee as you decide what role fasting will play in your committee:

1. How can fasting together help us in our work of selecting, training, and employing spiritual leaders?
2. What potential benefits might we gain by including fasting in our process of leadership development and training?

Holy Communion

Attendance at the Lord's Supper and engaging in regular times of worship is another essential discipline. All of our work in the church has the potential to be worshipful work. There is never a time or place where worship and celebration of the Lord's Supper is not appropriate. Celebration of Communion is a powerful way to remember the team nature of the church and to become an ever-expanding circle for those called into leadership in the local church.

Think about these questions:

1. How might the regular celebration of the sacrament of the Lord's Supper affect our committee?
2. How would our understanding of the work of the committee on lay leadership change if we were to begin every meeting, workshop, training, and evaluation with Holy Communion?
3. What benefits might be gained by setting all of our development and training work in the context of worship with Holy Communion?

Christian Conferencing

Christian conferencing, or conversation, is a hallmark of a community of faith. John Wesley acknowledged the joy of gathering together in Christian fellowship, but just enjoying one another's company is not enough. Taking time to talk about our faith—to ask others about their prayer life, their reading, their meditation, and their acts of charity and service—is a wonderful way of encouraging and supporting one another and holding one another accountable. The constant reminder of close Christian friends can help us greatly in our personal discipleship.

Consider using Christian conversation as the means by which evaluation can take place in your church. Reflect on these questions together:

1. How is it with the soul of our congregation?
2. How intentional have we been about prayer for ourselves? for others? for the world?
3. What gift have we made to another in the name of Jesus Christ?
4. In what ways have we done harm by commission or omission in the past month?
5. What opportunities to serve have we missed, and how might we more actively do good for others?
6. What have we read, learned, or heard that might lead us in a new direction?

If every one of our meetings began with a time for reflecting on the above questions, what changes might occur in the way we approach our tasks?

Concluding Thoughts

The very nature of our mission—to make disciples of Jesus Christ by reaching out and receiving people in the name of Christ, relating people to God, nurturing and strengthening people in their faith, and sending them into the world to live transformed and transforming lives—requires that we engage in acts of Christian mercy, charity, and service. Ultimately, the work of the committee on lay leadership is to enable people to live as the church every minute of every day of their lives. The congregation becomes the place where people can join their gifts and passions with those of others, and the work and will of God can best be accomplished.

Too often, our churches establish structures for ministry that become institutionalized. We develop a program and a schedule, and then we process people through the structure. We establish a way to worship and elect a worship committee to make sure everything works as planned. We establish a Sunday school and elect teachers to staff it. Rarely do we evaluate whether the structure and program need revision.

Jesus reminds us that "the sabbath was made for humankind, and not humankind for the sabbath" (Mark 2:27). The same can be said of the church. We do not *serve* the church; we *are* the church.

When the committee on lay leadership focuses on the people and the gifts that these people have been given by God, a new model emerges. The people who are elected to leadership have unique gifts, skills, knowledge, and passion. Together they share a vision and plan for ministry. From that unique and ever-changing perspective comes a plan for the best way to get the work done. We modify our processes and procedures to honor the unique gifts and personalities of the people.

The work of the committee on lay leadership is a vital ministry of the church. All too often we have placed people with the gifts of leadership or knowledge or administration on our lay leadership committee. While these characteristics are important, we also need people gifted with discernment, wisdom, shepherding, and prophecy to prayerfully find, develop, and equip God's leaders through our congregations. This is holy work. This is hard work. But this is the work that will enable our churches to grow beyond their institutional walls to become agents of change and spiritual transformation throughout the world.

Reflect on these questions:

1. How can our work empower the members of our congregation to live as Christian disciples seven days a week?
2. How can we design our discovery, development, and deployment processes to most effectively achieve our primary task?
3. How does our understanding of the work of the committee on lay leadership change when we think not in terms of electing people to *serve* the church but in terms of electing people to *be* the church?
4. How does this affect the scope of our work?

Endnotes

1 From *The Book of Discipline of The United Methodist Church—2000.* Copyright © 2000 by The United Methodist Publishing House. Used by permission; ¶258, page 162.

2 From *The Book of Discipline of The United Methodist Church—2000.* Copyright © 2000 by The United Methodist Publishing House. Used by permission; ¶258, page 162.

Chapter Four

Nurture Ministry Areas: Christian Education, Worship, Stewardship

Christian Education Ministry Area

The *Book of Discipline of The United Methodist Church* states that the "nurturing ministries of the congregation shall give attention to but not be limited to education, worship, Christian formation, membership care, small groups, and stewardship."[1] It further states that the church may elect leaders "who shall be responsible for helping to organize and supervise the total program for nurturing faith, building Christian community, and equipping people of all ages for ministry in daily life through small groups in the church."[2] In speaking of educational ministries it goes on to say, "In each local church there shall be a variety of small-group ministries, including the church school, for supporting the formation of Christian disciples focused on the transformation of the world. These small groups may concentrate on teaching and learning, fellowship, support, community ministries, and accountability. Members of small groups will build their knowledge of the Bible, the Christian faith, The United Methodist Church, and the societal context in which the church finds itself. In addition, small groups, including the church school, shall provide people with opportunities for practicing skills for faithful discipleship."[3]

With this kind of responsibility it is easy to see how the education ministry team should be a setting for team members to deepen their own relationships with God as they focus on helping the congregation grow in faith and discipleship. Each team meeting provides an opportunity to "practice what you preach." As you determine the settings that you will offer to children, youth, and adults for study, worship, fellowship, and service, you can also study together, experience the joy of being the body of Christ, worship, and find meaningful opportunities to serve your community as well as your congregation.

Scripture Study

Each meeting of your team might include a fifteen- to twenty-minute biblical reflection and conversation related to an aspect of your work. Consider the possibilities on pages 49–51. Each chart relates to a different area of your work.

	Team's Work: Nurturing Faith
Scripture	**Questions for Reflection**
Deuteronomy 6:4-9	1. What does this passage tell us about the depth and breadth of our task? 2. How do we help our congregation love God with all their heart, soul, and might? 3. In what ways are we equipping adults to share the stories of our faith with children and youth?
Psalm 25:1-10	1. What does this passage tell us about God? 2. What does it mean to "wait all day long" for God (verse 5)? 3. What does God need to teach our congregation (verses 5, 8, 9)?
Matthew 28:18-20	1. What do you think it means to "make disciples"? 2. What is the connection between baptism and the formation of disciples? What does it mean for our congregation when we pledge during a baptism to live according to the example of Christ? 3. How do our small groups help children, youth, and adults remember that Christ is "with you always" (verse 20)?
Luke 10:25-42	1. How do these two stories inform our understanding of the Great Commandment (to love God and neighbor as self)? 2. What can we learn from Jesus' teaching methods in his encounters with the lawyer and with Martha? 3. In what ways do our small groups help people love God and neighbor?

Team's Work: Building Christian Community

Scripture	Questions for Reflection
Joshua 24:1-18	1. What does Joshua's narrative tell us about the nature of God? 2. How did these stories form the Israelites into a community? 3. How does our congregation build a corporate memory of stories and symbols?
Isaiah 42:5-9	1. What does it mean for God to have "called you in righteousness" (verse 6)? 2. How does the concept of covenant inform our understanding of Christian community? 3. What "new things" are springing forth in our community and/or congregation?
John 15:1-12	1. What does it mean to "abide in" Christ? 2. What sort of "fruit" is evident in our congregational life as we learn to abide in Christ? 3. How do our small groups help children, youth, and adults love one another?
1 Peter 2:4-10	1. What does it mean to be "God's own people" (verse 9)? 2. In what ways do our small groups contribute to our congregation being "built into a spiritual house" (verse 5)? 3. In what ways have you experienced God's grace and mercy recently?

Team's Work: Equipping for Ministry in Daily Life	
Scripture	**Questions for Reflection**
Micah 6:6-8	1. What does it mean to "do justice, and to love kindness, and to walk humbly with your God" (verse 8)? 2. What knowledge do children, youth, and adults need to live out their faith? 3. What skills do children, youth, and adults need to live out their faith?
Matthew 25:31-46	1. How does this parable define the life of one who seeks to follow Christ? 2. Who are the hungry, sick, and lonely in our community? 3. What opportunities do we provide for our congregation to serve our community and the world?
Romans 12	1. What does it mean to be "transformed by the renewing of your minds" (verse 2)? 2. What are the characteristics of a community that is centered in Christ as defined by this chapter? 3. How is our congregation as a Christ-centered community helping people connect their faith with their daily lives?
Ephesians 4:1-7, 11-16	1. How is our congregation discerning the "calling to which you have been called" (verse 1)? 2. In what ways are we helping people discover their spiritual gifts? 3. How are our small groups "building up the body of Christ" and helping people grow in maturity (verses 12, 13)?

Prayer

Certainly each team meeting should include a time of prayer for your congregation, your pastor(s) and staff, your teachers and small-group leaders, and your team. As you plan for new classes, for special events such as vacation Bible school or a family retreat, or for how you will staff small-group ministries during the coming year, you will want to bathe each of these ministries in prayer. Prayer helps you remember what you want to accomplish and helps you align your plans with God's plan for your congregation.

In addition to opening or closing your team meeting with prayer, you may want to include a specific time for sharing joys and concerns, particularly those related to the team. Afterward you will want to spend some time in prayer. If you are dealing with a difficult situation in your congregation, you may want to offer prayers of petition, intercession, and confession. As team members report on the progress of particular ministries, you might offer prayers of thanksgiving or petition.

And remember, these prayers may be verbal, silent, spoken, sung. One team member may pray on behalf of the team. At other times, you may want to give each team member an opportunity to pray. You can use written prayers from resources such as *The United Methodist Book of Worship* or *Alive Now!* (see pages 94 and 95). These prayers may be read together or as a litany.

Acts of Compassion

As a team you will most likely plan opportunities for mission and outreach at various points during the year. These may vary from summer work camps for youth to Sunday school classes making Thanksgiving and Christmas baskets for families in need. Some congregations routinely participate in outreach projects such as providing shelter for homeless people, providing food or clothing for families in need, or tutoring children in an after-school program.

Any outreach projects such as these are opportunities for members of your small groups to be in service in Christ's name. They are also opportunities for your team to be involved in hands-on ministry. As you get to know your team members, you will discover the particular gifts and interests each has. These gifts and interests will point you in the right direction for responding to the needs in your community.

Christian Conferencing

Finally, as an education/nurture team, you are partners with the pastor and other ministry groups in leading the congregation's journey of discipleship. In your meetings you will want to consider what God is calling your congregation to be and to do. What does that mean for corporate worship? What does that mean for your small-group ministries? How will you communicate the goals of your ministry to the congregation and community?

Your responsibility does not exist in a vacuum. You plan your ministries within the context of your community, your state, your nation, and the world. Pay attention to the particular trends that are affecting participation in your ministries. Talk to members of the congregation and community to discover what issues they are facing. Read the newspapers and listen to the news. Create opportunities for feedback on the ministries you provide for learning and growing in faith. Find out what is working well and what needs to be improved. Then discuss this information with the team during your team meetings and decide what your next steps need to be.

In this way you will be participating in what John Wesley called Christian conferencing, a corporate means of grace in which you can discover God's presence in your midst, renew your commitment to live as disciples of Jesus Christ, and discern where God is leading you next as you continue to plan and evaluate effective small-group ministries. Indeed, one could make a case that an effective team meeting in the church is Christian conferencing at its best. As you develop these meeting skills, you will find your work together to be life-giving, meaningful, and joyful.

Worship Ministry Area

A congregation is a warm, living community—an organism. Its life is centered in the life and work of Christ with varied focal points: nurture, outreach, and witness. We frequently use terms like *evangelism, worship, stewardship, Christian education*, and *social concerns* to describe these areas. As a leader in the area of worship, your team invites people to pay attention to God in distinctive ways. Some of the primary ways are

- gathering in the name and praise of the triune God;
- reading and proclaiming the Scriptures;
- responding to the good news of Christ;
- forming people into a life of discipleship;
- entering into the joys and anguish of the world through communal prayer;
- celebrating Holy Communion;
- sending people out for ministry in daily life.

As the leader of the worship ministry team, you have been chosen to lead the worship leaders into the deep places of the Spirit so that together they are attentive to God both in the task of worship and in the task of being disciples. What if you and those on the worship ministry team were to agree that your first commitment will be to live as disciples together in this small group, and that out of that experience and discipline you will seek ways to lead and explore vital worship in the congregation?

This resource has already explored the means of grace in general ways (see Chapter 2). Here we will suggest specific ways to use the means of grace in leading the worship ministry team in spiritual formation. The spiritual formation of your group will be stronger if you take time to engage in two or more of the following during your time together. Consider meeting at least monthly.

Scripture Study

Begin your time together with an approach called divine reading, or *lectio divina*. This approach moves beyond an intellectual study of the Scriptures and will help your team listen for God's message to you. The chart below suggests Scripture passages that relate to worship.

Scripture	Guidance for Reflection
Isaiah 2:1-4, a vision of worship in the last days	Use for any of the listed passages.
	1. Read the text aloud. Ask, "What word or image stands out for you?" Allow a time of silence. Then invite each person to give his or her response without discussion. A basic rule: No interruption and no comment are needed. Just listen. The point is to listen deeply, not to discuss.
Isaiah 6:1-8, our response to the awe-inspiring presence of God	
Isaiah 58, God's rejection of worship disconnected from justice	
Amos 5:21-27, God's rejection of worship disconnected from justice	2. Ask another person to read the text aloud. Ask, "What invitation is here for me?" Repeat the silence, answering, and listening process.
Luke 4:16-21, the good news read in the synagogue	3. Ask a third person to read the text aloud. Ask, "What is the invitation for our worshiping community?" Repeat the silence, answering, and listening process.
Luke 19:29-39, the yearning of creation to welcome Jesus Christ	4. Transition to the task-completing part of the meeting with a time of prayer that incorporates some of the insights and awareness of the reflections.
Luke 24:13-35, telling the story, breaking the bread, recognizing the risen Lord	
Acts 2:41-47, the community feasting and living by the means of grace	5. Return to the insights, words, and phrases of this reflection time as it connects with and informs the work of worship in your congregation.
Revelation 4:1-11, the worship in heaven	

Holy Communion

Agree that team members will each keep a journal of participation in Holy Communion. Share the entries at each meeting. Ask that team members reflect on what actions in the service touched them or illumined their attention to God.

Ask the pastor to preside at a celebration of the Lord's Supper with your entire group around the table. Keep it short and simple, but let there be gathering, proclamation, prayer for others, and use of the Great Thanksgiving before partaking in the bread and cup. Invite everyone to raise their hands up and out at head level at the invitation, "Lift up your hearts."

Discuss with the team: What would it mean for people to actively remember God's mighty acts in Jesus Christ and to offer themselves in praise and thanksgiving as a holy and living sacrifice in union with Christ's offering for the life of the world?

Prayer

Informal Prayer

This is extemporaneous prayer, or what Wesley called praying extempore. This prayer is the breath of our spiritual life. It increases faith and love, opens us to God's gifts, and helps God's priorities become our priorities.

If your group is unfamiliar or uncomfortable with spontaneous prayer, try a circle of prayer. Invite each to name something he or she is thankful for or in need of. Then ask each to pray aloud or silently for the person on his or her right. Start the process yourself. Model and urge a single, simple sentence at first. If a person chooses to pray silently, he or she can squeeze the hand of the next person to indicate that he or she has finished offering prayer. Reflect together on the experience. Practice it together over the span of several meetings. Ask the group what they think might happen in corporate worship if worshipers were invited to form circles of three or four and engage in spontaneous prayer.

Written Prayers and Hymns

John Wesley also practiced reading and praying written prayers and other texts from the church's tradition, believing that this practice was a means of expanding his vocabulary and his awareness of the story and character of God. All of us get into ruts of prayer when left to our own composition. Pray together using prayers or appropriate hymns that can be found in *The United Methodist Hymnal* or *The United Methodist Book of Worship* (see page 95). Allow for silence following each. Reflect on how the range and awareness of God was expanded by this practice.

Reflect on the following questions with your ministry team:

1. How does our congregation relate to written prayers?
2. How could use of such prayers be powerful and transforming?
3. Can a case be made for some prayers being used frequently and repeatedly?
4. In what ways does the heart and mind need a memorized repertoire of prayers and hymns to fall back upon in times of trial and temptation?
5. What are the prayers, hymns, and liturgical texts our people now know and treasure?
6. What are the prayers, hymns, and liturgical texts our team would like to introduce as basic for our faith community's use?

Christian Conferencing

Wesley used the terms *Christian conference* and *watching over each other in love* to describe shared discipline and support. The General Rules of the church provide something to hold on to in a slippery world (see *Book of Discipline—2000*; pages 48–49, 71–74). When Christians don't have a rule and a group for support, it is easy for us to excuse ourselves for having compromised, abandoned, or otherwise denied our commitment to be Jesus' disciples in our daily life.

Read the lead sentence of each of the three rules on pages 73 and 74 of *The Book of Discipline—2000*, then silently look at the specifics under each. Ask the group to consider the following questions:

1. What keeps you from "evangelical living"?
2. Would having a group covenant shaped around the General Rules make a difference in the way we live as disciples?

As a group, consider creating a simple covenant or rule of life that you will live by, and for which each person will give an account each time the group meets. You can find more information on developing a group covenant in the book *Guide for Covenant Discipleship Groups* (see page 94).

Acts of Compassion and Acts of Justice

Wesley and the Anglicans referred to acts of compassion and justice as the works of mercy. How does worship in your church witness to the coming reign of God? If it is divorced from God's call for compassion for the suffering and those crying out under oppression, is it true worship?

Discuss the following with your team:

1. What suffering or oppression are we aware of in our community?
2. What actions are we as individuals taking, or what actions do we long to take, to welcome God's rule and deliverance in any of the circumstances just named?
3. What gets in the way of your being present in compassion and justice where these hurts and injustices exist?
4. Read and reflect on Amos 5:21-27 or Isaiah 58. How could weekly worship more fully connect with God's mission

> to bring good news to the poor . . .
> . . . to proclaim release to the captives
> and recovery of sight to the blind,
> to let the oppressed go free,
> to proclaim the year of the Lord's favor.
> (Luke 4:18-19)

What does it mean to worship God, who is in mission and sends us to be apostles where there is longing for hope, love, and justice?

Staying Centered on Christ's Work

Getting the job done is what your group is accustomed to doing when it meets: committees get tasks done. As those who practice attentiveness to God by centering acts at the beginning of your gatherings, your team can continue to practice that attention to God as you live in awareness of the work you are called to do. The former consciousness informs and transforms the latter.

You as the leader can practice this and invite the group to be aware of living and working at two levels at once. One way to do this is to call attention to it as you transition into the tasks on the agenda, and then to invite reflection in a time of closing and evaluation, asking the following:

1. How were you aware of the presence of the Spirit in our work together?
2. Were there times when we seemed to have forgotten the presence and power of the Holy Spirit among us?
3. What evidence was there that the Spirit was guiding and forming the way we worked together?

You can model attentiveness to the Spirit at any time in the meeting, and you can call the group to awareness of insights, reflections, and commitments made in the opening time or in previous meetings as they relate to the task work of the worship team.

Stewardship Ministry Area

Stewardship is a word that means many things to many people. It is a word used by biblical scholars and by business consultants. When church finance committees use the word *stewardship*, they are usually talking about a financial campaign. In this resource, we are using the word in a more biblical sense that has its roots in the first book of the Bible.

In the Creation story, God gave Adam and Eve responsibility to take care of all that is. They were invited to tend the garden (Genesis 2). God calls us to be faithful gardeners. We are invited to share our energies, our gifts, and our resources with God and with all of God's creatures and creation. That is what it means to be a steward.

Another meaning of stewardship is generosity. The Christian steward tills the garden of relationships by generously sharing time, abilities, influence, self, and resources. We want to encourage this generosity, not only of our finances but also of spirit, hospitality, energy, and passion. A primary responsibility of the stewardship ministry area is to encourage every dimension of generosity in all of its height, breadth, and depth. We will explore this beautiful expression of the faith through the lens of Scripture, experience, reason, and tradition.

Generosity becomes part of the ethos or spirit of the church where there is a dream and a team. Without a dream, generosity is only an abstract concept. A dream gives direction to generosity. In addition, a dream has magnetic attraction that draws other dreams from the hearts of the people. But the dream goes nowhere without a team; and unless the community of faith shares the dream, it is only an idea. The Holy Spirit is present "where two or three are gathered" (Matthew 18:20).

Reflect with your team on the following questions:
1. What are the ways we till the garden as individuals?
2. What are the ways we can till the garden as a ministry team?
3. What are the ways we till the garden as a congregation?

Biblical Roots

The word *generous* and its derivatives are found over thirty times in the Bible. A person who is generous can focus on what is important. Generosity in prayer is the commitment to tune out the distractions in order to communicate with God about important people, decisions, and experiences. Generosity in giving is the decision to invest one's resources in those things that are important rather than to carelessly spend money on the unimportant stuff that tempts us.

We are all stewards. The question we have to answer is, What kind of steward will I be? Jesus told parables about good stewards, dishonest stewards, and careless stewards. A steward can take care of relationships, of the creation, of an organization, of possessions. Some of us are better stewards in one area than in another. But God wants us to be generous with all we are and all we have.

The story of the Exodus is a helpful example of generosity, specifically the generosity of God. As the Israelites wandered through the wilderness, God provided them with manna. They had enough for each day, but no one could hoard any. The manna story provides a challenge to our North American culture's drive for accumulation. God has provided enough; but when we try to amass too much, it turns rotten. God's generosity is in providing enough rather than in our amassing huge amounts.

The next great biblical example of stewardship is the Exile. Jeremiah offered practical advice to the exiles, who found their lives in chaos after being forcibly removed from their homes and taken to Babylon. In Jeremiah 29, the prophet pleads with the discouraged group to settle down, buy land, raise gardens, have families, and tell the stories of what God has done. He is encouraging the exiles to focus on what is really important, to bring order out of chaos. A generous steward is one who makes time for family and invests time in prayer.

In the New Testament, the thrust of the Hebrew stories can be gathered under the umbrella of grace. "God so loved the world that he gave" (John 3:16). There is an abundance of grace (Romans 5:12-17). We are to be good stewards of God's generous grace (1 Peter 4:10). When Paul urged the Corinthians to contribute money to help the needy in Jerusalem, he started by saying, "We want you to know, brothers and sisters, about the grace of God that has been granted to the churches of Macedonia" (2 Corinthians 8:1). Further along in that same fundraising letter, Paul goes on to say, "You know the generous act of our Lord Jesus Christ . . ." (verve 9). Ultimately, a Christian's generosity is rooted in the biblical story of God's grace. That grace is most visible in the gift of Jesus.

Experience

When people describe the most important people in their lives, they nearly always speak of those who "gave themselves" in some way. The treasured memory is of a person who took time, showed interest in the person, or exhibited values that impressed the life of the individual.

If we examine our own lives, most of us find that we experience more satisfaction from sharing with others than from gathering things to ourselves. It is essential to spend time in prayer and discernment in order to sort out what is important. Without our intentionality toward determining what is important and making those things our first priority, urgent matters squeeze the important matters out of our lives.

Reflect with your ministry team on the following questions:

1. Name someone who has influenced your life and Christian journey through the giving of himself or herself. What and how did that person give?
2. In what ways do you give of yourself?
3. How would it affect the ministry of the stewardship team if we focused on giving of ourselves as a church?
4. How can we know what God wants us to be and to do as a ministry team? as a church?
5. (Spend time in prayer, including listening.) What is our really important work to do as a ministry team right now in our particular setting?

Reason

In some ways, generosity is not reasonable. Reason is shaped by the mental constructs and by the culture. The call to be faithful stewards is a call to root our reasoning in the long haul rather than in the immediate circumstances. In many ways, such thinking is counterrational. It is not irrational, but it starts the reasoning process from a different foundation.

For the Christian, reasoning is built on faith rather than faith being constructed out of our rational minds. God is the initiator. We are not the creators. All reasoning is rooted in certain presuppositions. Among the most important are the values that are the foundations for our lives. If those values are not rooted and grounded in God's revelation, we affirm that the house is built on sand.

Tradition

Throughout the long history of the Christian faith, generosity has been seen as a way for a person to connect with God and with others. In fact, connections with one are not possible without connections with the other. In the account of the Last Judgment, Jesus said, "Just as you did it to one of the least of these who are members of my family, you did it to me" (Matthew 25:40).

Many of our traditions have their roots in biblical stories. The story of Naomi and Ruth includes a story of traditional generosity called gleaning. Farmers left some of the crop in the field so that those without food could gather something to eat. Throughout the whole history of the Christian church, individuals and churches have explored ways to show concern and provide help for the poor and the hungry.

In the modern era a variety of traditions about financial giving have arisen. In many African churches, the time of offering is a great celebration accompanied with singing and dancing. In Pacific Island congregations, there is an annual celebration of ingathering where people share their offerings with great joy. In some North American congregations, people bring their offering to the Communion rail when they "offer themselves" to receive the bread and the wine.

One of the great traditions of generosity is the tithe. You can learn more about this ancient tradition in the book *Holy Smoke! Whatever Happened to Tithing?* (see page 95).

Reflect with your ministry team on the following questions:
1. What are the giving traditions in our church?
2. What is the connection of these traditions to the biblical faith and ancient practices?

Practical Implications

Stewardship is something that one should be about all year rather than for only three weeks in the fall. It is about generosity, but the generosity is inclusive of the whole of life. Paul told the Corinthians that they were "stewards of God's mysteries" (1 Corinthians 4:1). Consider ways your congregation can be a more faithful and effective steward of the gospel.

Generosity is a central factor in relationships. When a church asks for more and more volunteer time from people and doesn't encourage them or help them to be stewards of their relationships in the home, the church is not encouraging stewardship. Consider ways your congregation can help family members give their time to one another as well as to God's wider family of people.

Generosity is in response to the generous God who brought hope and redemption to the whole world. Are all of your church's invitations to give related to faith? Does the offering in worship help people connect their lives to the God of love? Explore ways to invite people into generosity that are consistent with the biblical story of God's generosity.

What do you affirm in your church? Do you affirm people who use their gifts and graces only within the organization, or also those who express their discipleship in their jobs, their homes, their neighborhoods, and other settings? Do you affirm only the more visible church tasks, like singing in the choir and ushering, or do you also affirm those invisible tasks that are essential for the church's ministry? Affirm groups and individuals who express a wide variety of generous actions.

What is celebrated by your church? Can you celebrate the news of growing churches in Africa and the Philippines? Can you celebrate the homeless receiving food, and battered women having shelter? Is the offering a time of celebration, or is it only a perfunctory act? Guide your congregation in keeping vigilance for things to celebrate.

Scripture Study

At the beginning of your meetings read and study one of the following Scripture passages, which were discussed on pages 60 and 61 under "Biblical Roots." Use the questions in the chart below to help your team reflect upon the biblical and theological foundations of stewardship. Spend time reflecting on the questions as they relate to the lives of the individuals on the team. Reflect also on the questions as they relate to your life and work as a team.

Scripture	Questions for Reflection
Exodus 12:33-42; 16	1. What does the Exodus story say to us in our personal lives? 2. How do we relate stewardship and generosity of our resources to the concept of amassing hoards of goods? 3. How does the story of the Exodus inform our work and decisions as a stewardship ministry team? 4. How does the story of the Exodus inform the decisions we make as a church?
Jeremiah 29:1-14	1. What would it mean for us to seek the welfare of our community? 2. How does the story of the Exile relate to our church and the way we use our resources?
John 3:16; Romans 5:12-17; 1 Peter 4:10; 2 Corinthians 8:1-6; 2 Corinthians 9:9-12	1. How do we offer grace through our decisions as a stewardship ministry team? 2. If we took grace seriously, how would it affect the way we make decisions around the use of financial resources?

Christian Conferencing

The reflection time is a significant way in which your team will engage in Christian conferencing. Such Christian conferencing will help the ministry team keep your work focused on Christ as you plan and make decisions.

Prayer

Spend time in each meeting in prayer. Use this as a time for team members to lift up personal joys, concerns, and other prayer needs. At the beginning of the meeting, look at the biblical passages or theological statements you will be reflecting on. In those passages, what are the issues of stewardship that relate to your work as a team and congregation? Pray for those concerns.

At each meeting, spend time praying for specific issues related to the way your team and congregation understand stewardship and live out of the understanding of generosity talked about here. Include in your prayers concerns for your community and for the world. Look through *The United Methodist Hymnal* for the many prayers that will help keep your team focused on their ministry.

Holy Communion

Holy Communion is an important part of our life together as a Christian community. There may be times during the year when it is important for you to take Communion together as a team, perhaps as you begin your work together as a new team or as you approach significant celebrations in the Christian year.

Conclusion

Stewardship is an act of the individual and of the community. We are all stewards. The question is whether we, both individually and as a church, are faithful stewards or unfaithful stewards. Stewardship is more than placing money in an offering plate. It is the way we as individuals spend our time, our energy, our influence, and our resources. And it is the way the church as the faith community spends its time, energy, influence, and resources.

Stewardship is not a fundraising technique but a faith-raising journey. One important aspect of that faith journey is sharing. Thus generosity is one aspect of growing in faith. Whenever generosity is separated from faith, the church becomes focused on the budget rather than on faith, justice, and mercy. Whenever generosity of time is reduced to filling committee functions, we have violated the gracious invitation of God to use our giftedness with joy.

Be good stewards of the faith and of your resources as you help those in your church find Jesus Christ as Lord over every other aspect of their lives and communities.

Endnotes

1 From *The Book of Discipline of The United Methodist Church—2000.* Copyright © 2000 by The United Methodist Publishing House. Used by permission; ¶251, page 152.

2 From *The Book of Discipline of The United Methodist Church—2000.* Copyright © 2000 by The United Methodist Publishing House. Used by permission; ¶254, page 155.

3 From *The Book of Discipline of The United Methodist Church—2000.* Copyright © 2000 by The United Methodist Publishing House. Used by permission; ¶255, page 156.

Chapter Five

Outreach Ministry Areas: Restorative Justice

The *Book of Discipline—2000* states that the "outreach ministries of the church shall give attention to local and larger community ministries of compassion, justice, and advocacy."[1] One way a church can give attention to these concerns is through a ministry area on restorative justice. While this chapter deals specifically with restorative justice, the basic concepts for spiritual formation within the life of the ministry area can be applied to other outreach ministry areas.

What Is Restorative Justice?

Though the language of restorative justice may be new to many of today's United Methodists, it is a concept deeply rooted in our Scriptures and in tribal and agrarian traditions on several continents. The basic idea is that when a crime (understood as someone violating another) has taken place, it is the victim, the offender, and the local community who are the greatest stakeholders and who know best what needs to happen for the situation to be made right.

The retributive criminal justice system now in place is based on blaming, punishment, and revenge. It marginalizes all parties involved, giving decision-making power to professionals such as lawyers and judges acting on behalf of the all-powerful state. In contrast, restorative justice has a healing focus and seeks to empower the primary stakeholders to deal with their conflict by dealing with one another through dialogue and negotiation, trying to discern together what the victim needs, who is responsible, and how the offender and the community can work together to make it right. Accountability then becomes the offender taking responsibility for his or her offense and making it up to the victim as far as possible rather than passively accepting punishment while the victim—and the relationship between the offender and the victim—goes unrestored. This often means that the offender makes restitution to the victim through money and/or labor. It sometimes also means that the offender offers service to the secondary victim, the local community.

Restorative justice cares about both victims and offenders and brings them together rather than separating them, all in the historical, economic, political, and religious context of their lives and the life of the community. This means that the community must also shoulder its share of responsibility by helping the offender get what he or she needs to make a better life, and by addressing whatever systemic problems—economic, political, and so forth—may have contributed to the crime.

Restorative justice is not a program, though its values and principles are expressed in victim-offender mediation programs in the United States and elsewhere. Rather, restorative justice is a perspective, an approach to crime, conflict, and human relationships. It is a way of life as much as it is an alternative, community-based way of doing criminal justice. As such, it has strong foundations in the biblical witness as well as in our Wesleyan tradition.

Scripture Study

As a congregational leader in restorative justice ministries, you will want to help your team explore biblical passages through a restorative justice lens. As you do this, new dimensions of meaning will open up, and new levels of spiritual discernment will reward the group. Consistently beginning each team meeting with prayer and Bible study from this restorative justice perspective can highlight the personal and theological aspects—the spiritual dimension—of the work the committee is called to do.

Perhaps the oldest Bible passage having direct relevance for restorative justice ministries is the introduction of the year of jubilee in Leviticus 25. This passage and the many passages articulating the concept of *shalom* (right relationships, peace with justice) throughout the Old Testament make clear several key principles of restorative justice. These include (1) that spirituality is relational, not just individualistic; (2) that God's justice is not the same as our justice, and that God's justice and God's love are not separate but together; and (3) that what is called distributive justice (how wealth, power, and status are divided among groups in a society) must not be separated from what we understand as criminal justice (how a society responds to crime). The Hebrew prophets, notably in Isaiah 58 and 61, have reaffirmed these same messages. Micah 6:8 spells out in clear terms the inseparability of humility from one's relationship with God, the inseparability of mercy and kindness from one's relationships with others, and the inseparability of doing justice from one's relationships with society.

In the New Testament, key passages underlying restorative justice include Matthew 5–7 (the Sermon on the Mount, in which Jesus radicalizes and deepens the Law and calls for a nonviolent, nonjudgmental response to evil); Matthew 18:15-22 (where Jesus lays out a restorative justice process for conflicts within the church and tells his followers to forgive infinitely); Matthew 25:31-46 (where our fate is linked to whether or not we respond to the suffering of those in prison and elsewhere); Luke 4:16-30 (where Jesus claims to embody the jubilee command, including the liberation of those in prison); Luke 10:25-37 (where Jesus clearly teaches that the victim is a neighbor, whom we are to love even at cost to ourselves); John 8:2-11 (where Jesus confronts the death penalty by turning the question upside down to ask if anyone deserves to carry out the execution); and 2 Corinthians 5:16-21 (where Paul lifts up reconciliation as God's work through Jesus and as our work).

It is important that a local church ministry area on restorative justice be well-grounded in Scripture. The way of restorative justice is not the way of the world, and it is easy to get seduced into the old, failed model of retribution and revenge. Here, as everywhere, the church is called to be countercultural, to witness to God's transformation of the world. This requires spiritual discipline.

Use one of the Scripture passages and the guidelines in the chart below to focus your work in Christ.

Scripture	Guidance for Reflection
Leviticus 25:8-55 Isaiah 58 Isaiah 61 Micah 6:8 Matthew 5–7 Matthew 18:15-22 Matthew 25:31-46 Luke 4:16-30 Luke 10:25-37 John 8:2-11 2 Corinthians 5:16-21	Use for any of the listed passages. 1. Begin the meeting by reading through the passage or selected verses. Ask the team members to listen for a word or image that stands out for them. Discuss these reflections together. 2. Read the passage again and ask how it relates to the individual team member's life of discipleship. 3. Spend time as a team discussing what this means in relation to the ministry of your team and to the outreach ministry of the congregation. Discuss: If we were to take the passage seriously, would it make a difference in the way we engage in ministry through the church or in the community? 4. You may use the same passage in more than one meeting, continuing to ask how it relates to the individual team members' lives of discipleship and ways of making decisions, and what it means to your team ministry and the ministry of your congregation in specific areas.

Prayer

After you have reflected on Scripture passages, spend time in prayer, sharing concerns and joys related to those passages as well as listening for God's guidance for the work of your team. Discuss: For your team and your congregation, what is your ministry related to outreach ministries in your particular setting? Listen for God's guidance. Silence is part of your life of prayer, individually and as a team. Pray for the ministries you are involved in and the people you relate to through those ministries. Pray for specific concerns related to restorative justice in your community.

Acts of Compassion and Acts of Justice

It is hard work to keep the balance between being supportive of someone and holding someone accountable. It is equally hard to let oneself be supported by and held accountable by the same person. But this is exactly what offenders—who include all of us sinners—need, and what restorative justice must do. If you think about it, this is also what Jesus did with his disciples and what God does with all of us. It is a spiritual discipline and a means of grace for a community of faith to give to and take from one another in the spirit of mutual support and mutual accountability. In a sense, to offer support is an act of compassion, and to hold accountable is an act of justice. Both are vital to restorative justice.

Spend time with your ministry area discussing how you will support one another and how you will hold one another accountable. The goal is to have a situation where the internal life of the ministry team mirrors what the group is working on. The rhythm of listening and speaking, of confronting and responding, of confessing and (in some measure) forgiving—that is, the rhythm of justice and love—characterizes both the life of the team and the essence of what it is trying to bring about in the world in the arena of crime and our society's response to it.

Another way to consider the importance of acts of compassion and acts of justice is to acknowledge the twofold nature of ministry.

In restorative justice, as elsewhere, the ministry of the people of God (and not just the ordained ones!) must be holistic. It must include the ministry of presence, of personal relationship, of hands-on service. These are acts of compassion and works of mercy: comforting crime victims, visiting those in prison, binding up the wounds of the broken and the brokenhearted. Church people are traditionally pretty good at these acts.

But it is no less important for the church, and for those working for restorative justice, to be about the acts of justice. This means that we must engage in the ministry of advocacy, the ministry of community organizing, the ministry of political struggle (which can also be spiritual struggle). In moving into these difficult and often thankless tasks, we are following not only the Hebrew prophets but also the Lord Jesus. The Hebrew prophets spoke truth to the powerful and afflicted the comfortable in their oppression of others. The Lord Jesus told the scribes and Pharisees who they were; overturned the tables of the moneychangers in God's Temple; and confronted the religious, political, and legal establishment of his time and place most directly in his trial and execution.

Restorative justice is not just about restoring some kind of harmony in a particular case or relationship. It is most essentially about transforming an unjust system into a truly fair, compassionate justice system for victims, victimizers, and local communities. And this necessitates controversy, conflict, and politics, which are full of spiritual tests.

Reflect with your team on these questions:

1. How are acts of compassion and acts of justice also acts of support and accountability?

2. How are we giving support and holding one another accountable for our planning and work as a ministry team?

3. How are we giving support and holding people accountable as we participate in restorative justice ministries in our community, either with individuals or with organizations and groups?

Christian Conferencing

The only way we can find and sustain the strength to do the work of restorative justice in a Christian spirit is, again, to live and work together within a context of prayer, Bible study, discernment, mutual support and accountability, and Christian conferencing. Christian conferencing is a way of doing business in which we as a church listen to both the context in which we are working (such as the crime and punishment arena) and to our faith community and our larger human community. We do this through continuing Bible study, prayer, and theological discourse.

Again, we see a parallel with restorative justice itself. One of the most exciting methods of doing restorative justice is for the victim, the offender, close family members and significant others of each, and important local community figures to come together for discussion, discernment, and deliberation over what crime has taken place and what should be done about it. This process takes place according to a few simple guidelines and under the guidance of a trained facilitator, and it attends closely to feelings as well as behavior, to the future as well as the past, and to relationships as well as laws that were broken. Often the outcome includes not just what the offender agrees to do to make things right with his or her victim and the community but also what the community must do together to prevent recurrence of similar violations. Restorative justice practitioners often call this process family group conferencing. In a secular society, such events are usually not, and shouldn't be, examples of Christian conferencing. But they can nevertheless be informed by a spiritual dimension and be influenced by those Christians who take part.

Reflect on these questions with your ministry team:

1. How can Christian conferencing change the way we plan and do our work together?

2. How can Christian conferencing change the way we live our time together as a ministry team?

Endnote

1 From *The Book of Discipline of The United Methodist Church—2000*. Copyright © 2000 by The United Methodist Publishing House. Used by permission; ¶251, page 153.

Chapter Six

Witness Ministry Areas: Evangelism

Witness and *evangelism* are words understood in a variety of ways. Evangelism is not what we do *to* people. It is the sharing of good news—specifically the good news of Jesus Christ. Many people think of an evangelist as a person who preaches or has an extraordinary faith story to share. But all disciples of Jesus Christ are called to share the ways their God makes a difference in the decisions they make, in the kind of relationships they have, and in the lifestyle they live. The congregation is also an evangelist, one who shares good news. The ethos, or culture, of the congregation can be one in which people experience God's love. If the congregation offers biblical hospitality and welcome and is a place where people experience God's love and hear words of hope, healing, and wholeness, that congregation is witnessing and evangelizing.

If the evangelism ministry team is to (1) equip members of the congregation to share their faith in their everyday lives and (2) nurture the congregation to become a place of biblical hospitality, then it is important that the team meetings themselves are places of faith formation for the members. The work of the team is not about completing a set of tasks but about asking, What does God want us to be and to do in this particular time and place? How can we most effectively help our faith community be a place where people experience welcome and safety because they experience God's love and grace through the members of our community?

Scripture Study

Keeping biblical reflection and prayer as foundational in your time together will help you discern what God would have you do and be. The charts below through page 80 suggest biblical passages and reflection questions that can be used during your meeting.

Team's Work: Sharing Faith and Witnessing	
Scripture	Questions for Reflection
Luke 15	1. Reflect on the actions and attitudes of the one who is searching. 2. What are our feelings about those who do not have a relationship with God through Jesus Christ and who are "lost" in our world? Do we really believe that a relationship with Jesus might make a difference in their lives? If so, what are we doing as a church to live out that belief? 3. What difference would it make in our life as a ministry team and in the life of our congregation if we really believed that it is important that people have a relationship with Jesus and that it will make a difference?
John 1:35-46	1. What is the relationship between the person who shares faith and the one being invited to meet Jesus?

	2. What are the common elements between the story of Andrew and Simon Peter and the story of Philip and Nathanael? 3. What do these stories tell us about whom we might share faith with? about what we might share? 4. What do these stories tell us about equipping people to share their faith?
John 4	1. What in the story indicates the excitement of the woman as she goes to tell what she has experienced? 2. What is the relationship of the woman to the people she is going to tell? What are their feelings toward one another? 3. What does this passage tell us about the way our faith affects the way we see people? What does it say about our church's outreach to people?
Acts 3:1-10; 4:13	1. Where were Peter and John going, and why is that important in the ministry of faith sharing? 2. What was the man asking for? What are some possible reasons he was asking only for alms and not for healing? 3. What did Peter and John do that showed they valued the person? 4. What do you think prepared Peter and John to be able to really see the man and not just pass him by? to truly value the person and not just treat him as an object? 5. What does this passage tell us about nurturing our own faith? What does it tell us about the ways we are called to relate to all people with the good news?

Team's Work: Hospitality	
Scripture	**Questions for Reflection**
Genesis 18:1-15	1. What did Abraham offer to the strangers? What did Sarah and Abraham receive? 2. In what ways do we offer the best that we have to visitors in our congregation? 3. Reflect on a time when you offered hospitality to someone you did not know well and received an unexpected gift in return. 4. When has our church offered hospitality and received an unexpected gift in return? 5. What difference would it make if we related to each person we meet as someone through whom God can offer a message or a gift?
Matthew 25:37-40	1. In what ways does our church welcome people? In what ways does our church reach out to people? Where are the places Christ might say to our congregation, "As you have welcomed these, you have welcomed me"? 2. What would you as individuals do differently and how would your attitude be different if you knew that every person you met, whether inside the church or outside, is someone to be welcomed and treated as Christ?
Romans 15:7	1. How has Christ welcomed each of us? 2. What difference would it make if each person in our congregation welcomed those who entered as Christ welcomed them? 3. How can we help members of the congregation offer that kind of hospitality?

Christian Conferencing

One of the ways we grow in our own faith is through listening and storytelling. We participate in Christian conferencing as we talk with one another about our relationship with God and what difference that has made and continues to make in our lives. Perhaps your group could begin the first few meetings by asking each person to tell about a person who influenced his or her faith journey, using the following questions:

1. Who is one person who influenced your faith journey?
2. What was it about the person, or what did the person do, that made a difference?
3. What does this tell us about who we are and how we might mentor others?
4. How does this remind us of the importance of integrity of faith expressed in words and life lived? How does this help us as we look at the work of this ministry area?

Prayer

Include a time of prayer in each meeting. Be sure to pray for local, national, and global situations currently in the news. What specific issues in these situations relate to sharing the good news with people in God's world? Include some of those concerns in your prayers each meeting in addition to the prayer concerns of the team members. What specific concerns relate to evangelism, welcoming, hospitality, discipleship, and ministry of your local church?

There are a variety of ways to pray in meetings. Use prayers from *The United Methodist Hymnal* or other sources. Mention the area of concern and invite people to pray silently or aloud as they choose. Spend time listening for God and waiting on God as you move into the planning and decision-making time in your meeting. When you ask "What is God calling us to do?" and "Who is God calling us to be?" listen for God's voice in the Scripture as well as in prayer.

Team members can also participate in individual prayer organized through the team. Ask each person to make a list of four people in his or her network of relationships who are not actively involved in a church. Ask that each person pray for the four people on the list daily for a month, then to invite the four people to a worship service or a small-group experience in the church.

All team members need to participate in congregational worship services and Communion services as part of their own spiritual formation. There may be significant times during the year when you also want to have Holy Communion together as a ministry team, such as your first meeting together or as you approach Easter, Pentecost, Advent, or other times of special planning.

Acts of Mercy and Compassion

Acts of mercy and compassion are not unrelated to the evangelism ministry team. The culture or personality of the congregation serves as evangelist. Observe how your congregation expresses God's love toward people outside and inside the church. Whom do you invite? Observe, then spend part of a meeting focusing on how you can express mercy, compassion, and hospitality to all people, particularly those immediately surrounding the church building.

Discuss the following:

1. Do we express welcome differently depending on the way people dress, wear their hair, or express themselves?

2. How are we expressing compassion and mercy to all members of the congregation?

3. Are there differences in the way we treat some people? If there are differences in the way we treat people who are "different," strangers, or not "like us," are there issues of justice in our congregational system that need to be addressed?

Section Three
Staying Focused

You are a spiritual leader who has responsibility for leading a ministry or administrative team. As a spiritual leader you see yourself on a journey of faith, seeking to know God more deeply. You are clear that the team for which you have leadership responsibility is more than a group of people with a task to accomplish. The task is important; it is vital to the life and ministry of the congregation. But your team is also a small group where faith formation takes place and where growth in discipleship happens. No matter what the task of your ministry team, the question your team must ask is, What does God want us to do and to be in this particular time and place?

Chapter Seven

Putting It All Together

Nurturing Your Own Faith

Because you are a spiritual leader, it is important for you to decide the role that the means of grace will play in your own spiritual journey. What feeds your soul the most? Is it silence and contemplation? Is it reading and gaining more information about the Scriptures? Is it reading the Scriptures, meditating, and journaling? Is it working at a soup kitchen or participating in Habitat for Humanity? How are you intentional about doing all the good you can and avoiding doing harm? Keep doing those spiritual disciplines that most help you to know God and to know about God. Also consider studying Scriptures in new ways or participating in spiritual disciplines that will stretch you and help you grow.

Nurturing Faith in the Team

What does it mean to grow in discipleship, for you as well as for the others on your ministry team or administrative team? If your small group not only has a task to complete but also is a place for faith formation, it will be a place where people are helped to keep the Great Commandment.

When the scribes pushed Jesus, trying to trip him up in his response to the question about which was the most important commandment, Jesus responded, "The first is, 'Hear, O Israel: the Lord our God, the Lord is one; you shall love the Lord your God with all your heart, and with all your soul, and with all your mind, and with all your strength.' The second is this, 'You shall love your neighbor as yourself.' There is no other commandment greater than these" (Mark 12:29-31). This is what our faith journey is about: learning to love God more deeply and learning to love our neighbor.

How can we help those on our team grow in these relationships? How can we look at the work and ministry we have to do and ask if the decisions we are making reflect loving God and loving neighbor? What would our time and relationships, our interactions, look like if we loved God and loved neighbor? While Ephesians 4 has a broader context, read the following as though it has to do with the relationships of the people on your team as you relate to one another and work together:

> So then, putting away falsehood, let all of us speak the truth to our neighbors, for we are members of one another. Be angry but do not sin; do not let the sun go down on your anger, and do not make room for the devil. Thieves must give up stealing; rather let them labor and work honestly with their own hands, so as to have something to share with the needy. Let no evil talk come out of your mouths, but only what is useful for building up, as there is need, so that your words may give grace to those who hear. And do not grieve the Holy Spirit of God, with which you were marked with a seal for the day of redemption. Put away from you all bitterness and wrath and anger and wrangling and slander, together with all malice, and be kind to one another, tenderhearted, forgiving one another, as God in Christ has forgiven you. Therefore be imitators of God, as beloved children, and live in love, as Christ loved us and gave himself up for us, a fragrant offering and sacrifice to God. (Ephesians 4:25–5:2)

Has there ever been disagreement within the ministry team or administrative team to which you are giving leadership? Sometimes there is disagreement; sometimes misunderstanding. Sometimes we do not even know why we hold so tightly to an idea, so tightly that we can only argue our point and not really hear the other person's point of view. Sometimes we believe that there is only one way to accomplish a specific task, and hard feelings are created. What does it mean for us to have disagreements but to live and work in Christian community in our team so that we can forgive others as Christ forgave and forgives us? Living together in Christian community as we do our work and ministry together means that we guard what we say about and to one another. The Scripture invites us to be imitators of God in our relationships.

Developing a Covenant

Even ministry teams and administrative teams may find it helpful to develop a covenant about how they will live in Christian community as they do their work together. In the midst of planning and discerning what God would have the team do and be, how will the team members live together so that they will experience the graciousness of God?

Gabriella, Michelle, Bryan, and Tom were on the Nurture Ministry Team at South Valley Church. They were all used to being in the public eye, being assertive, making group decisions by talking through the issues, and putting forth ideas in a group whether or not those ideas became part of the final plan. Bill, Chuck, and Vicki, also members of the team, were not as comfortable talking in a group. Because they were not as used to participating in such a setting, they were slower to express their thoughts and ideas. It took them longer to think through the options that were available.

Therefore, the team included in their covenant that they would listen to one another, value what each person had to say, be respectful of one another, be careful not to interrupt one another when they were talking, and encourage input from all members of the team. They agreed that they would not talk about one another after or between meetings, and that if they had any question or issue that was not understood or was unresolved, they would go directly to the person to ask for clarification. In this way they would uphold the idea, "Let no evil talk come out of your mouths, but only what is useful for building up, as there is need, so that your words may give grace to those who hear" (Ephesians 4:29).

Part of the covenant included caring for one another. That meant that they would provide a time during each meeting for sharing words of joy, thanksgiving, or need for personal concerns, for the work of the team, for the church, and for the world. Being able to share briefly about personal concerns and joys enabled the group to support and encourage one another. It also meant that they were better able to understand one another.

The covenant was designed to develop a trusting relationship where the members were able to hear one another with caring and honesty, living out that "we are members of one another" (Ephesians 4:25). Isn't it true that once we have developed a relationship of trust, we listen more intently and with different "filters" that help us work and live together differently? What would your covenant look like if you took the Great Commandment and the Ephesians passage seriously for your work and life together as a team?

Another component of the example group's covenant was holding one another accountable. They agreed to a beginning and ending time and dates for the ministry gatherings. Each person said yes to full participation in the discussion, work, and planning of the times together for formation and ministry. And each person was invited to help hold the others accountable for carrying through with what they said they would do and for keeping the original covenant.

They also agreed in the covenant that they would pray for one another between meetings. What are the other components in a covenant that will help your ministry team, administrative team, or other leadership team in the local church grow in discipleship by personal and corporate participation in the means of grace?

A covenant is developed, signed, and held before the group. This process has nothing to do with keeping the law; it has everything to do with growing together in love and Christian community. It has everything to do with modeling together what Christian community is in other small groups, in the family, and in the community. It has everything to do with how we live and share ministry together in such a way that we are imitators of Christ as we share the good news and participate with God in God's world.

Opportunities for Faith Sharing

One of the ways caring grows within a group is by team members having an opportunity to share their faith in the group. Sharing faith is done in a variety of ways. It happens when we have an opportunity to tell how God, through Christ, made a difference in our faith journey.

Laurel was a member of a worship ministry team that read a Christmas Scripture about God coming to be with us, to stand with us. The group paused for reflection. In those moments, Laurel, who had felt so alone for so many years, was overwhelmed with the idea that God was standing with her in life. Tears came to her eyes. She noticed that she was not alone in that response, and the person next to her touched her arm. In that one moment, Laurel experienced God's presence through another person. Later Laurel was able to tell how that person was a channel through which she experienced God's gracious love. That was sharing her faith experience.

Tricia was on the nurture ministry team. The team was talking about the Scripture of the woman who had been bent over for years. As they discussed the story, Tricia talked about the time when she had felt so loaded down by circumstances in her life that she felt as though she could not get out from under the weight. It had distorted her view of herself as well as the world. God had touched her life and helped her to stand straight once again, getting a better perspective on who she was and how to see the people around her. Tricia shared her faith by telling about this experience in which God's story and her personal life story intersected.

Andy was a member of the stewardship team. The team was talking about the story of the ten lepers. All of the lepers were healed, but only one came back to say thank you to Jesus. Andy told how he felt that he took too many things for granted, both in his relationship with God and in his relationship with his family. Andy shared faith as he told of his struggle in being faithful in giving thanks.

Sharing faith helps us stay focused on God's activity in our own lives and in the meaning we find for everyday living in our relationship with God through Christ. It is a way of encouraging one another in the journey. It helps us clarify not only where we are now in our journey but also where we have been in that journey.

When we share our faith in ministry and administrative teams, it will probably not mean long stories from each person at each meeting. Most of the time it will simply mean having an opportunity to voice a concern or to reflect aloud on a passage of Scripture that is foundational for the work being done. Sharing our faith stories helps us know one another as real people who have strengths; who have questions and struggles; who have had significant growing moments in our faith journey; and who, no matter how strong and firm in the faith, have needs and concerns in life. It helps us know others as people we are called to encourage and support through our caring and prayers.

As moments of faith sharing take place, there is the possibility that real Christian community will develop. Sharing faith and faith stories may indeed help us stay focused, stay centered, on the Center.

Guidance From the Early Church

This book is not just about how to carry out the responsibilities of the team for which you are giving leadership. Many teams can begin that work by looking at *Guidelines for Leading Your Congregation*, a series of booklets designed to help leaders of specific ministry and administrative groups within the church explore some of the responsibilities that are assigned or implied through *The Book of Discipline* (see page 95).

Once you have looked at some of your team responsibilities, the question becomes how to take those responsibilities seriously in your own context. How do you work on your tasks in such a way that you are making decisions out of a biblical and theological foundation; out of lives that are centered in God through Jesus Christ; and in a way that team members, in your life together in Christian community, continue to be formed as disciples in the process.

Your team may find help in a chapter of this book written specifically for your team. In the various chapters are suggestions for the biblical and theological foundations that your team may want to explore as you do your work together. Also in those chapters are suggested ways that teams may participate together in the means of grace. If your particular ministry or administrative area is not represented in this book, you may still find ideas that will act as a catalyst for your own thinking and ideas related to the team you are leading.

Often groups find the Book of Acts helpful as a guide for study and prayer. You will find in the Book of Acts the ways that the early Christians tried to live out what it means to love God and love neighbor. You will see how they took their own devotional life seriously. You will see how they were called to specific ministries out of their own giftedness and experience. You will see how they faced real-life struggles and real-life human relations issues. And you will see how they came to make decisions out of a life of prayer and devotion, and how they made decisions based on the values that were the essence of who they were as Christians. The life and values out of which they made decisions about church concerns were not just a segmented part of their lives that they thought about and practiced when they were together for worship, study, and prayer. Instead, the worship, study, and prayer not only informed the decisions and actions of the church but informed and formed the lives of the community members.

As you lead your team, do you let the world's messages of consumerism, hoarding for self, lack of concern for what happens to others, and violence influence your decisions? Or do the stories and values of the Christian faith form the values that form and inform the decisions you make in your role as a leader? Look at decisions your team makes and ask:

- What message does that decision give?
- What are the values inherent in the decision?
- Are the values expressed in our team's decisions and actions resident in our Judeo-Christian heritage?
- What stories of our Christian faith, our denomination, our church, and our own faith journeys shape who we are and what we bring to the team community as we make decisions and action plans within and for our teams and churches, our communities, and the world?
- What language are we using as we talk about the issues before us? Does this language come from values of the world that are not in alignment with the values of the Christian faith, or does it come from values of the Christian faith?
- Will those who are influenced and affected by the decisions and plans of our team experience the graciousness of God? Will they experience the actions of people who are continuing to be formed in the faith and are, at least in many moments, imitators of Christ?
- Has the team, as a Christian community and as individuals, been formed in faith through the process of biblical and theological reflection as we have made this decision?

If we do not have biblical and theological reflection, if we do not remember and rehearse the stories of faith, if we do not open ourselves to receive God's grace through participation in the means of grace in these team settings, it is difficult for us to be shaped by the Word and by the faith. Every time we gather as a ministry team or administrative team, we gather as part of the body of Christ, as a small group where one of the goals is to be formed and transformed by God's grace. That grace can be experienced even in the midst of disagreements about how to approach an issue, even in the midst of tensions that may arise in relationships. It can be experienced, that is, if we understand ourselves as growing in loving God and loving our neighbor, who may even be those we are least in agreement with in our team!

Staying Focused

When you enter a place of worship, you get a sense about the culture of the congregation within the first few minutes. Your experience and presence in that place will tell you if it is a place of hospitality where you will experience the graciousness of God. You will know if you are welcomed, even as a stranger, or if you are considered an outsider. You will know if the church is for people already in that particular church or if it is for all people. Each congregation has a unique personality about it, a climate, a culture, an ethos, an essence of who they are at the core.

The same is true for church boards, ministry teams, and administrative teams within the church. The agenda that is established indicates much about what the team values. How does your agenda reflect your commitment to faith formation? Making sure that your agenda includes intentional time for prayer, Scripture study, and faith sharing will help establish a climate that reflects the importance of being formed into Christian disciples. Just stating your commitment in the agenda doesn't make it so, but it does remind the group of its guiding vision.

If your ministry teams and administrative teams are not already meeting with an understanding that they are small groups where Christian formation is taking place and where decisions are made based on biblical and theological foundations and reflections, know that change will probably not happen quickly. Stay focused! The team is part of the church, part of the body of Christ. We are on a journey together, and this is part of the journey.

The journey is individual; for out of our own life experiences and experiences of the means of grace, we each grow in our knowledge of God and our relationship with God. The journey is also corporate, as community is part of our Judeo-Christian heritage. That corporate journey takes place in small groups—small groups for study and prayer, small groups building homes for people with low incomes, small groups serving meals to the homeless, small groups called choirs, and small groups called ministry teams and administrative teams—as well as in the larger community that gathers for worship. All of those experiences influence the journey of both individual and community.

Stay focused on who you are as a community of faith. Stay focused on answering the question, Who does God want us to be and what does God want us to do in this particular time and place? Stay focused on the core values of the Christian faith and story. Stay focused on our center, Jesus Christ.

Helpful Resources

Alive Now! (The Upper Room).

Cultivating Christian Community, by Thomas R. Hawkins (Discipleship Resources, 2001).

Discover Your Spiritual Type: A Guide to Individual and Congregational Growth, by Corinne Ware (The Alban Institute, 1995).

Equipped for Every Good Work: Building a Gifts-Based Church, by Dan R. Dick and Barbara Miller (Discipleship Resources, 2001).

Grace Notes: Spirituality and the Choir, by M. Anne Burnette Hook (Discipleship Resources, 1998).

Guide for Covenant Discipleship Groups, by Gayle Turner Watson (Discipleship Resources, 2000).

Guidelines for Leading Your Congregation, 2001–2004 (Cokesbury, 2000).

Holy Smoke! Whatever Happened to Tithing? by J. Clif Christopher and Herb Mather (Discipleship Resources, 1999).

The Book of Discipline of The United Methodist Church, 1996 and 2000 editions (The United Methodist Publishing House, 1996, 2000).

The Christian Small-Group Leader, by Thomas R. Hawkins (Discipleship Resources, 2001).

The General Board of Discipleship website: www.gbod.org.

The Heart's Journey: Christian Spiritual Formation in the Life of a Small Group, by Barb Nardi Kurtz (Discipleship Resources, 2001).

The United Methodist Book of Worship (The United Methodist Publishing House, 1992).

The United Methodist Hymnal (The United Methodist Publishing House, 1989).

Transforming Church Boards Into Communities of Spiritual Leaders, by Charles M. Olsen (The Alban Institute, 1995).

Ordering Information

Resources published by Discipleship Resources may be ordered by mail at Discipleship Resources Distribution Center, P.O. Box 1616, Alpharetta, GA 30009-1616; by phone at 800-685-4370; by fax at 770-442-9742; or online at www.discipleshipresources.org.

Alive Now, published by The Upper Room, may be ordered by phone at 1-800-925-6847 (toll free) or 1-515-246-6917; or online at www.upperroom.org/alivenow.

Other print resources may be ordered from Cokesbury by phone at 1-800-672-1789; by fax at 800-445-8189; or online at www.Cokesbury.com.

About the Contributors

Daniel T. Benedict, Jr., is Director of Worship Resources for the General Board of Discipleship and is an elder in the California Pacific Annual Conference. Dan contributed the section on worship in Chapter Four.

M. Anne Burnette Hook was formerly Director of Music Resources for the General Board of Discipleship and is a deacon in the Memphis Annual Conference. Anne contributed Section One.

Shirley F. Clement is Director of Evangelism Ministries for the General Board of Discipleship and is a diaconal minister in the Wisconsin Annual Conference. Shirley contributed Chapter Six, on evangelism, and Section Three.

Dan R. Dick is Director of Congregational Planning and Leader Development for the General Board of Discipleship and is an elder in the Greater New Jersey Annual Conference. Dan contributed Chapter Three, on the committee on lay leadership.

Carol F. Krau is Director of Christian Formation and Spiritual Leadership for the General Board of Discipleship and is a diaconal minister in the Tennessee Annual Conference. Carol contributed the section on Christian education in Chapter Four.

Herb Mather is Director of the Center for Christian Stewardship for the General Board of Discipleship and is an elder in the South Indiana Annual Conference. Herb contributed the section on stewardship in Chapter Four.

Harmon Wray was formerly Director of Restorative Justice Ministries for the General Board of Global Ministries and is a layperson active in his local church in Nashville. Harmon contributed Chapter Five, on restorative justice.